D1616938

Jews in Romania 1866-1919: From Exclusion to Emancipation

Carol Iancu

Translated by Carvel de Bussy

EAST EUROPEAN MONOGRAPHS, BOULDER
DISTRIBUTED BY COLUMBIA UNIVERSITY PRESS, NEW YORK
1996

EAST EUROPEAN MONOGRAPHS, NO. CDXLIX

THIS VOLUME WAS PUBLISHED WITH
THE FINANCIAL ASSISTANCE OF
THE FRENCH MINISTRY OF CULTURE

Printed in the United States of America

BOOKS PREVIOUSLY PUBLISHED BY THE AUTHOR

Le Juifs en Roumanie (1866-1919). De l'exclusion à l'émancipation, préface de Pierre Guiral. Aix-en-Provence: Université de Provence, 1978. 382 pp.

Juifs et judaïsme en Afrique du Nord dans l'Antinquité et le Haut Moyen Age. Montpellier: Université Paul Valéry, 1985. 117 pp.

Armand Lunel et les Juifs du Midi. Montpellier: Université Paul Valéry, 1986. 360 pp.

Bleichröder et Crémieux. Le combat pour l'émancipation des Juifs de Roumanie devant le Congrés de Berlin. Correspondance inédite (1878-1880). Montpellier: Université Paul Valéry, 1987. 264 pp.

Les Juifs à Montpellier et dans le Languedoc. Du Moyen Age à nos jours, postface de Gérard Nahon. Montpellier: Université Paul Valéry, 1988. 446 pp.

L'Émancipation des Juifs de Roumanie (1913-1919). De l'inégalité civique aux droits de minorité: l'originalité d'un combat à partir des guerres balkaniques et jusqu'à la Conférence de paix de Paris, préface de Charles-Olivier Carbonell. Montpellier: Université Paul Valéry, 1992. 350 pp. (Prix de la Foundation culturelle israélienne.)

Le Combat international pour l'émancipation des Juifs de Roumanie. Documents et témoignages. Volume 1 (1913-1919). Tel Aviv: Diaspora Research Institute, 1994. 317 pp.

Les Juifs du Midi. Une histoire millénaire. Avignon: Ed. A. Barthélemy, 1995. 384 pp.

Permanences et mutations dans la société israélienne. Montpellier: Université Paul Valéry, 1996. 192p.

Les Juifs en Roumanie (1919-1938). De l'émancipation à la marginalisation, préface de Pierre Guiral, postface de Gérard Nahon. Paris-Louvain, 1996. 388 pp.

To the memory of my maternal grandfather,
Herşcu Moscovici,
killed in battle during The Great War,
and to my mother and father,
Clara And Iţic Iancu

CONTENTS

PREFACE

As far as one goes back into the history of the Jewish world, one finds more or less confirmed anti-Semitism. It was known in antiquity and was practiced in the Middle Ages. However, we must come to the twentieth century, to Hitlerism, before it acquired its quality of inexorable persecution, before the "final solution" made its appearance, that solution which spared no one, rejecting the good Jew and the converted Jew, mixing all Jews in the same gas chamber. But in spite of its dreadfulness which we do not deny, the way for Nazi anti-Semitism had been prepared in Eastern Europe and it was not by simple coincidence that Romania took the road to persecution and massacre earlier than others during the Second World War.

In fact, Romania is the subject of the fine book that Mr. Carol Iancu has published under the title *Jews in Romania (1866-1919): From Exclusion to Emancipation*. Note the dates! We follow the Jewish minority, a large minority, through its reconquest of Romanian nationality, its self-awareness, its struggles, its victory. To a great extent, there is nothing new in this conquest: it is related to a wide movement which has not stopped since the dawn of the present era; it is part of the right of nations to self-determination which was proclaimed by the French Revolution, aided by Napoleon III and confirmed by President Wilson. But this is where the paradox or scandal appears. On the one hand, Romania, like Greece, Serbia and Bulgaria, achieved its independence through harsh fighting; it became a state, with a ruler, a beautiful capital and politicians trained in the Western manner. On the other hand, it exercised deliberate, systematic anti-Semitism coming from above, even though it met with sympathy and indulgence from below. But these two phenomena were only superficially at odds with each other. In the middle of the nineteenth century, Prevost-Paradol, whose partly Jewish origins made him quite sensitive to such threats, noted that every national movement that succeeded tended to consider, and would continue to consider, the Jew as being of a different race - a foreign element. Let us add to that the density of population in Moldavia, the resurgence of Christian anti-Semitism, the jealousy of the bourgeoisie, the ambiguous policies of the Hohenzollern ruler, the diversion of politicians who thought that anti-Semitism was the easiest way to fend off public anger and to allay discontent. And of course the intellectuals and the clergy played their part in this concert which included all instruments and where all arguments were repeated.

If Mr. Iancu had restricted himself only to a precise analysis of the persecution, his book would be of genuine interest for that reason alone, but, with a wide range of diplomatic experience, he has shown that Europe, at least Western Europe, was not indifferent. France, and also Great Britain, defended the Jewish cause and we should also note the continuous generosity of Napoleon III to William Waddington, the French Plenipotentiary at the Congress of Berlin. Surprising was the beginning role of the United States, which was considerable. Above all, this refers to Benjamin Peixotto, who was appointed American Consul for the sole purpose of improving the condition of the Jews, but we believe more and more that history is made by active minorities and generous individuals. In any case, from the end of the nineteenth century, there have been two worlds facing the Jewish problem: that of Eastern and Central Europe and that of the West, a West that stretches from Paris to Cleveland.

This is still a new work. Mr. Iancu is the best qualified to carry it out. His knowledge of foreign languages, his lively curiosity, his feeling for humanity, both for the life of the farmer and the world of chanceries, makes him the historian worthy of this great subject. Thanks to him, a sad chapter in the history of this awakening Romania has again come to life. Of course, it is the history of a minority, but it is also the history of a country which is seeking to find its way, of a Europe which is divided, and of attitudes which we know too well had to have a sequel and an attempt at a "final solution."

Pierre Guiral
Director of the Center for Studies in
Contemporary Political Thought
University of Provence

FOREWORD

The present work, *Jews in Romania (1866-1919): From Exclusion to Emancipation*, is based, with a few changes, on my doctoral thesis, entitled "Anti-Semitism and the Emancipation of the Jews in Romania (1866-1919)," defended on June 17, 1976, at the University of Aix-en-Provence.

It might seem presumptuous to say that this study is indispensable. However, it is true that it was undertaken to fill a surprising gap. In fact, although anti-Semitism - one of the most astonishing and important phenomena of modern times - has become better known in Western countries and in Russia through the works of Jules Isaac, Jacob Katz, F. Lovsky, Léon Poliakov, Hannah Arendt and Shmuel Ettinger, among others, nothing had been done in the area concerning Romania. Such an undertaking also responded to the need to make the fate of the Jews in Romania and their struggle for emancipation known, if only in part, all the more so as the Jews have been excluded almost systematically from Romanian history since the Second World War.

Therefore, I have chosen to study the condition of the Jewish minority though analysis of the system of exclusion in that Carpathian country at a time that was crucial in its evolving statehood. I am aware of the emotional problems, to use the favorite term of Labrousse, arising from this subject. This is why it is appropriate to stress that, instead of following a deliberate point of view, the signs of hostility towards the Jews have been listed chronologically during moments of tension and crisis. They do not question the long tradition of tolerance by the Romanian people.

The idea of writing a thesis on the Jews in Romania (1866-1919) had its origin in a paper presented to the Hebrew University of Jerusalem in 1968, entitled "The Revolution of 1848 and the Jews in the Danubian Principalities."

In fact, the conclusions drawn as a result of this report called for more detailed research regarding the timing of the apparently determinist phenomenon called anti-Semitism. As mentioned by Léon Poliakov in his history of anti-Semitism, it has been determinist for the Christian and Moslem cultures, but does not exist in the Far East.

This is the paradox which had to be explained: How did it happen that the same persons who organized and directed the Revolution of 1848, who proclaimed equality in civil and political rights for their "Jewish brothers," became the promoters of official persecution against the Jews after becoming ministers and prime

ministers in the governments of Prince Carol? For what reasons did
they later evade the political emancipation of the Jews demanded by
the Congress of Berlin, which was even a condition for the international recognition of Romania, and then also degrade their status
by transforming them from natives into "foreigners not protected by
a foreign power?" How can one explain the growth of anti-Semitism
after 1878, when ever wider sectors of the Jewish population were in
the process of assimilation?

Why was there so much resistance towards recognizing the
Jews as citizens with equal rights, thus making Romania one of the
last countries in Europe to emancipate its inhabitants of Mosaic
religion at the end of the First World War?

In order to reach an understanding of the facts, which are at
first glance not only revolting but illogical, I have tried to make an
overall study of the relations between the Jews and the people amidst
whom they lived.

I have tried to make this study with research in the various
libraries and archives of Israel, France and Romania. It owes much
to the teaching of my professors, Michel Confino, Shmuel Ettinger,
Jacob Katz, Baruch Mevurah, Yaakov Talmon of the University of
Jerusalem, as well as to the intellectual effervescence that reigned
there before and after the Six Days' War.

But this thesis would certainly never have been written without
the outstanding direction, the brilliant advice, and the confidence
given to me by Professor Pierre Guiral. I trust he will find here the
expression of my deep gratitude.

From his research, courses and seminars I learned methods of
research appropriate for a French university. Thus, the way of
dealing with this subject derives from that double filiation. That
made me all the more responsible and it is with a feeling of awe that
I have set about the writing. Nevertheless, I have written this thesis
with a genuine care for objectivity, although aware that it is impossible to be impassive in historical matters.

First of all, it is a pleasant duty to express thanks to Messrs.
Jean Poliatchek and Claude Vigée, who made it possible for me to be
acquainted with France through a scholarship from the French
government.

During my study, I made the acquaintance of many persons
who helped me with their knowledge and goodwill. I have a real
moral debt to Louis Cohn, Alex Derczansky, Georges Haupt, whose

brutal death stunned all of his many friends, Herbert Maza, Gérard Nahon and René Strat. I also owe much to the late lamented Professor Constantin C. Giurescu of the University of Bucharest for having given me useful bibliographical information; and to Rabi who received me earlier in his Tolstoyesque house at Briancon and made me aware of the ambiguities of life in the Diaspora today; to Madame Lévine of the library of the Universal Israeli Alliance, and to those in charge of the many archives, libraries and centers of documentation who helped me to gain access to the treasures they protected.

The assistance of Madame and of our late lamented Léon Lipschutz was of great help, for in their home I found as much friendship as erudition.

I am grateful to Daniéle Iancu, in the springtime of my French period, who typed the first manuscript of this study and encouraged me at difficult times. For her perseverance, I shall say to her, borrowing from the words of Jeremiah (II,2): "I remember thee...when thou wentest after me in the wilderness, in a land that was not sown."

This book was published with the financial assistance of the following organizations and individuals whom I deeply thank: the Zadoc Kahn Association, the Elie Cohen Foundation, the Jacob Benveniste Foundation, the Central Consistory of French Jews, the B'nai B'rith Association, Cote d'Azur Lodge 1625, the B'nai B'rith Association, Emile Zola Lodge and Hermann Mayer.

Aix-en-Provence,
Spring, 1976 to Spring, 1978

INTRODUCTION

The history of the Jewish people in the Diaspora (i.e., dispersion) is constantly troubled by powerful centrifugal and centripetal forces. The centrifugal forces remove the Jewish individual from his traditional environment and project him into a surrounding society in which he loses his special character and disappears as such sooner or later. This is called assimilation. On the other hand, the centripetal forces bring the individual back from the periphery, from assimilation, from the failure to recognize one's own personality, to the bosom of his original milieu.

One of the most important centripetal forces in modern times is anti-Semitism. By its reverse effect, it has resulted in the case of individuals in the awakening of certain scholars of Jewish history who have become a Pandora's box. It was because of anti-Semitism that completely assimilated Jews like Theodor Herzl, Bernard Lazare, and Jules Isaac, to only name three outstanding examples, returned to Judaism and acted as they did.

At a collective level, this centripetal force has brought about a phenomenon whose expansion became universal from the time of its modern inception: the Jewish national movement, political Zionism. Not that the Jewish conscience, as Hannah Arendt has pointed out, has even been a simple product of anti-Semitism, and she has rightly criticized the myth of Sartre-type existentialism which defined the Jew as one who was deemed to be so by others. For, since the Babylonian exile, the constant concern of Jewish existence has been survival as a *people*.

Yaakov Talmon, in an excellent essay on the unicity and universality of Jewish history, compares the destiny of a nation with that of a person and points out that it may be the result of a trauma in early childhood or the outcome of a fundamental experience. He says: "The Jewish psyche underwent a traumatic deformation because of the terrible shock to Jewish belief in their being chosen caused by the national catastrophe and exile. That shock made most Jews impervious to the assimilating influences of Hellenism and Rome."

Although the preservation of the Jews as an identifiable entity under diaspora conditions was for eighteen centuries the result of a *deliberate separation* and not one forced upon them, it is certain that in the nineteenth and twentieth centuries, after emancipation and the generalization of assimilation, anti-Semitism played, and still plays, a part in the preservation of that people.

How has that centripetal force shown itself in Romania, in that region of Eastern Europe which apparently lies outside any system of Occidental criteria and which has earned for itself over many years the label of being "the classic anti-Semitic country?" This is the question I asked myself before beginning this study, which is an attempt at a psycho-historical interpretation both as regards the Jews and anti-Semitism.

A systematic history of the Jews in Romania has not yet appeared. There are quite a few monographs, but no overall study based on archival research. The work we have envisaged is part of a broader project in the framework of those monographs which should culminate in a genuine history of Romanian Judaism.

A few words are needed about the tools which were at our disposal for beginning this study. The basis of our research lies in a systematic analysis of the collections of four archives: the archives of the Universal Israeli Alliance, the archives of the Ministry of Foreign Affairs, the General Archives of the History of Israel, and the Central Zionist Archives.

The press of the period was an important field of research for our subject: we have studied publications in several languages, especially Romanian. This study, which was made at the National and University Library of Jerusalem, at the Library of the Universal Israeli Alliance, at the Bibliotheque Nationale in Paris and at the Library of the Romanian Academy at Bucharest, is much less systematic for two reasons: we have had to make a choice amidst the mass of newspapers and were rarely able to find, or have access to, complete series.

I was also interested in the reports of debates in the Romanian Parliament on the status of the Jews at important moments in the history of the country. I made careful reading of works and evidence bearing on this subject.

For time-limits, I have chosen 1866 and 1919. The first date is that of the ascension of a foreign prince to rule the country: Carol Hohenzollern-Stigmaringen, and of the writing of a constitution which provided that only Christians could hold Romanian citizenship. The second is the culminating point in the long struggle of the Jews to enter the Romanian community, the attainment of rights as citizens through political emancipation.

This is a key period both in the history of modern Romania and the history of the Jews, and of anti-Semitism in so far as it appears as an integral part of the European movement. To explain the breadth of the anti-Semite movement, we have used the "line of development" as described by W. H. Burston in *The Principles of History Teaching*, published in London by Methuen in 1963. Using this method, we have tried to organize the existing material and to present it as the (partial) Holocaust of the Romanian Jews during the Second World War, or the end of a long process in the growth of hatred towards the people of Israel. The fact that from the time of their attainment of power, the Romanian fascists were responsible for the bloody pogroms - the most glaring of which was that of Jassy of June 29 and 30, 1941 - and that out of the approximately 400,000 Romanian Jews killed during the war (in 1930 the Jewish population was 760,000), 265,000 were the victims of the fascist government and part of the population, can only be understood in the context of this historical perspective of the development of anti-Semitic ideology which had become a real doctrine of the country after having been propagated among the masses a half century earlier.

We do not hold an eschatological view of history and it is not our intention to explain the socio-political alienation of the Jews in the second half of the nineteenth century and the beginning of the twentieth by genocide. But we cannot omit the events which were to take place scarcely half a century later of which premonitory signs were quite clear. The congested world of Moldavia was indeed the tragic but logical result of a phenomenon which reached its paroxysm and crystallized towards the end of the nineteenth century into a general movement that progressed and grew in an alarming way.

However, the same period of the Holocaust causes the historian to face this troubling question: how can one explain that, in all of the countries occupied or controlled by the Nazis where the Jewish population was nearly destroyed, half succeeded in surviving in Romania? This survival was due to many factors brought out by Theodore Lavi which must have upset many of the myths held by a number of Jewish intellectuals today. Raul Hildberg, Bruno Bettelheim and Hannah Arendt, using inadequate sources, claimed that if the Jews had resisted, implying that they did not, the number of survivors would have been greater. In addition, they declared that without the Jewish organizations and their leaders, the chaos would have been enormous, with many victims, but the total would never have reached six million (including 1,800,000 children). In other words, instead of resisting extermination, the Jews contributed to it with their own hands. Hannah Arendt says in *Eichmann at Jerusalem*: "The thing that is most unclear is not the bestiality of the SS members, but the part played by the Jewish leaders in their people's death."

What happened in Romania constitutes a formal rejection of all these allegations. The Jews survived above all through their own struggle, conducted by their leaders at every possible level. But if half of the community of Jews was saved from genocide, it was because there was an area where the Jews could unfold their efforts. Opposed to the destructive anti-Semitic movement, there was a strong current that rejected their solution to the Jewish question. Without a doubt, the very nature of that current must be sought in the economic, cultural and psychological conditions of Romanian society before the Second World War. But these two trends, this ambivalent attitude towards the Jews, already existed at the period we are studying and that is where I intend to direct my research.

Of course, certain objections may be made to the choice of this method of approach, because it is my purpose to treat the subject from the viewpoint of non-Jewish society towards the Jews.

But I have also analyzed the reaction of the Jews, especially when that reaction was extremist: political Zionism. Besides, the latter movement can only be presented in its deep organic interaction with the former.

What are the characteristics of Romanian anti-Semitism? What was its impact on Romanian society between 1866 and 1919? What was the real nature of the Jewish community and which were the key moments of its history? We have tried to answer these questions as clearly as possible from the viewpoint of events as we saw them. We have adhered to the chronological order required by this kind of investigation in considering the different facets studied.

My thesis deals with a phenomenon and a society which are little known or are ignored in the West. But because of the very nature of the subject, the range of problems we are studying is not especially of one period or one kind of society. Thus it is normal that certain facts that form an integral part of a history of events give rise to parallels and comparisons.

Just as an event which is deeply rooted in the history of a country, as, for example, the French Revolution, cannot be looked upon as a special, isolated, national event, but must be studied in its interdependence on other middle-class revolutions, so also anti-Semitism in Romania in the second half of the nineteenth century can only be considered in close relationship with similar performances in other countries. Taking this analogy further, it seems to us that the "chain revolutions" of the period from 1770 to 1850 which changed the structures of the Western world and extending as far as Central and Eastern Europe can be applied to anti-Semitism as a spatial (European) and temporal (modern) movement.

But there is an important difference between the manifestations of this phenomenon in the second part of the nineteenth century, in the countries where Jews were living legally (Central and Western Europe) and those where they had not yet been emancipated (Eastern Europe). Even in the former, political equality of the Jews did not take place simultaneously and it met with strong resistance. In fact, although the Constituent Assembly in France proclaimed the emancipation of the Jews on September 27, 1701, it was not finally accepted in England until 1860, in Germany until 1864 (it existed earlier in certain states), in Italy until 1866 and in Austria-Hungary until 1867. Prior to emancipation, anti-Judaism in those countries was primarily juridical: legislation concerning the Jews had come from Roman law and the canon law of the Church. In the first half of the nineteenth century, Jews were excluded from state service, as the latter was still considered to be deeply Christian. With emancipation, it was hoped that there would be complete integration of the Jews in a society which was moving towards secularization and that anti-Semitism would disappear. But those hopes did not materialize. For the Church, the emancipated Jews became the symbol of its defeat, whereas they had played no part in the battle between the old world and the new; it was through them that it started the struggle against the secular state. A doctrinaire anti-Semitism grew up in a series of pamphlets in which the classic accusations (deicide, Satanism, usury) were complemented by new themes (nation, race, revolution). It was not the monopoly of churchmen; representatives of other classes and trends of opinion enriched it with masterpieces of hate and folly. Hannah Arendt even declared that all classes of society became anti-Semite. She wrote: "Every class of society which had come into conflict with the State at one time or another became anti-Semite, because the Jews were the only social group which seemed to represent the State."

This conclusion derives from the simultaneity of the rise and fall of the nation-state and the Jewish communities of Western and Central Europe. The plan was simple: prior to the French Revolution, the nation-state evolved in the shadow of absolute monarchies. A number of Jews emerged from obscurity, becoming businessmen, princes and the financiers of government transactions. They were the "Court Jews" (*Hofjuden*), who enjoyed great privileges. After the Revolution, when the nation-state arose in the modern meaning of the term, the governments need for money became steadily greater: larger groups of capitalists had to be addressed and so the privileges previously granted only to the Court Jews were extended to all who were emancipated. But in the second part of the nineteenth century, the extraordinary expansion of capitalism eliminated the financial influence of the Jews at the government level. The beginnings of economic imperialism marked the decline of the nation-state which provided the latter relative security while taking advantage of their services. What was their new situation? On the one hand, they became the scapegoats of all the classes which were in conflict with the State. On the other hand, as a result of emancipation and assimilation, they were also threatened from within: their Jewishness was becoming secularized or Christianized. It seemed as though the Jews were about to be eliminated from the society which had previously de-Jewicized them. But in fact, this new anti-Semitism reawakened Jewish consciousness and played the centripetal role of which we spoke before.

The legal status of the Jews was everywhere accompanied by abolition of laws restricting them. Under those circumstances, anti-Semitism as an ideology or as a movement (political party) was expressed in writings or in a political way. But the aim of the anti-Semites in their press or in parliamentary action was to reenact the old laws of discrimination, to expel the Jews or annihilate them outright. This tendency was quite clear in Germany, where a petition signed by 225,000 persons was brought forward in 1880 asking that Jews be quarantined. It demanded their exclusion from public office, particularly from judgeships and from teaching positions. It had no immediate result, but in 1901 the Bavarian Diet passed a law limiting the number of judges of Jewish origin in Bavaria. The breadth of anti-Semitism in the West may be measured by the Dreyfus Affair which represented a real crisis in the French national conscience under the Third Republic. It was the result, not the occasion, for that passionate debate on the Jewish problem.

However, in spite of these outbreaks and many others, the juridical situation of the Jews did not change, and their social, cultural and political promotion (especially the latter after 1848) continued without obstacles.

Different from Western European, where anti-Semitism had more political than economic cause, the contexts in which it developed in Romania and Russia (including Poland) were not all the same.

In those countries, anti-Semitism was openly practiced by the governments and unleashed expressions of extreme violence. Russian anti-Semitism began with the introduction of the system of pogroms, that of Romania with xenophobic legislation which struck at the Jews without even naming them explicitly. In both countries, the Jews were placed under laws of exception and justice was inseparable from the Orthodox Christian religion. But whereas freedom did not exist in Russia, in Romania it was proclaimed by the constitution and it was through a trick, as we shall see, that the Jews were excluded from enjoying civil and political rights. While Western societies were becoming secularized, in those countries the Church, with its teaching of scorn, to use the classic phrase of Jules Isaac, remained the pillar of the state. But it was economic, social and demographic factors which characterized and shaped the explosions of hatred against the Jews.

Whereas the anti-Semitic phenomenon in Russia may be explained by the specific conditions of that country, which we do not intend to study here, in Romania the facts of what became the real Jewish problem in the second part of the nineteenth century are different.

The Principalities of Moldavia and Wallachia which made up Romania in the second half of the last century experienced an eventful political development with which we shall deal in the first chapter. That political change, brought about at the end of the Phanariot regime (1711-1821) by events as important as the Organic Law imposed by the Russians in 1834, the Revolution of 1848, the union of Moldavia and Wallachia in 1859, the Treaty and Convention of Paris in 1856 and 1858, the election of Carol Hohenzollern-Sigmaringen and the promulgation of the Constitution of 1866, had important repercussions on the situation of the different classes of Romanian society, including the Jews. The latter, whose origins go far back in the history of the country, underwent a considerable demographic increase at the end of the eighteenth and in the first half of the nineteenth century through the immigration of Jews from Galicia and Russia. That immigration, widely encouraged by the princes and the boyars, led to the creation of small localities in Moldavia called *targuri*, or small towns, which functioned as centers for the exchange of merchandise. In a society which was essentially agricultural, the great mass of the Romanian people was made up of farmers, dependent on a small number of powerful landlords, the *boieri* (boyars). The intermediate role between the two classes was largely filed by the Jews in Moldavia and by the Greeks and Bulgars in Wallachia.

The growth of the economic part played by that middle-class coincided with the last phases of the century-old struggle of the Romanians to survive and achieve unification as a nation. The awakening of Romanian nationalism in the nineteenth century was accompanied by an explosion of xenophobia whose victims were foreigners in general and Jews in particular. The measures taken against the Jews at the time of the Organic Law, which later changed into a struggle towards annihilation of the Jewish element, confirm this point of view. Did this mean that the phenomenon of anti-Semitism was solely the result of the impossibility of bringing this extreme nationalism into harmony with economic requirements and the liberal ideology borrowed from the West, which itself went far beyond the half-feudal stage of Romanian society?

This was my hypothesis prior to consulting religious and juridical sources going back as far as possible into the history of the Principalities. In fact, it seemed clear to me, and I wanted to be convinced, that there was no trace of oppression in this country which had already received those expelled from Spain and where so many immigrants had found refuge in later centuries. But great was our surprise when, after much reading, we had to accept the evidence: written anti-Judaism existed as early as in the old laws of the Romanian countries at the beginning of the seventeenth century. The tradition of the teaching of scorn and the classic accusations were present in other European countries. That is why we cannot agree with the theory of Joseph Bercowitz that anti-Semitism was essentially a Russian importation. But it is nevertheless certain that the legislation of the Organic Law had ill-omened consequences with respect to the situation of the Jews. It sowed confusion between the status of native Jews present in the country for generations and those who had recently immigrated and were under foreign protection, a thing which was common at that time even for Romanians who wanted to avoid in that way the arbitrary decisions of the tax authorities. From then on, the Jews were all considered together, like a nation - which was true, for, by their own customs, language, dress, cultural environment, they were quite different from the rest of the population - but a foreign nation, thus discriminating against the native Jews. Besides, instead of encouraging their assimilation, through a whole series of regulations the Jews found themselves not only excluded from political life but even from civil life itself: they were prohibited from living in the countryside, gradually excluded from most of the liberal professions, catalogued and treated like aliens. Despite the promises of civil and political equality in the revolutionary proclamations of 1848, their situation continued to deteriorate.

As a result of the Crimean War, the Paris Conference (1856) decided that the interior organization of the Principalities would be made according to the wishes of the Moldo-Wallachian populations represented by national assemblies called *ad hoc divans*. The Wallachian *divan* did not consider the situation of the Jews; the Moldavian one demanded not giving political rights to the Jews.

In spite of the Treaty of Paris of 1858, which provided for the enjoyment of civil rights by Moldo-Wallachians without distinction of religion, the Jews were shut out of the privileges of native citizens. The Jewish question became a parliamentary issue under the new constitution and the electoral law of 1866 which gave political power to the young Romanian middle-class.

The era of exclusion began with the new regime which was installed in 1866: henceforth the persecutions were sometimes brutal, sometimes hidden, but they were always legal. The relentless opposition to the Jews stemmed from both the boyars and the new bourgeoisie. As long as the Jews fulfilled their role as all kinds of intermediaries, such as tax collectors and sellers of liquor, of which the boyars held the monopoly, the latter tended to grant them some privileges, but when the Jews showed their will to combine with each other, to obtain civil and political rights, they were called a social danger. It was economic conditions which incited the hatred of the young Christian bourgeoisie. In fact, the Jews, who had been the pioneers of urban development in Moldavia, found themselves placed as much by circumstance as by vocation in a professional structure where trade and handicraft were preponderant. After their expulsion from the countryside in the late 1870s, there began a process of demographic concentration in the cities, but also a strong professional concentration of the Jews: certain areas of trade and of handicraft became their monopoly. To this was added upward social mobility and an ideological concentration which crystallized in two movements: socialism and Zionism. These three manifestations - professional concentration, upward social mobility and ideological concentration - were not limited to Romania and Saul Friedlander outlined their almost universal scope in the developments of modern anti-Semitism in his book, *Nazi Anti-Semitism: History of a Collective Psychosis*, published in Paris by Editions Seuil in 1971.

In the context of Romanian sociology, we must take account of another phenomenon which is as important as it is original. Fearing for its position, the land-owning aristocracy long persevered in preventing the normal development of a middle-class. That was why they encouraged the Jews to assume the intermediary positions.

Even before the end of the nineteenth century, the underdevelopment of Romania led to the first anti-Semitic organizations. The governments were unable to solve the serious agrarian problems and give a minimum of equality and justice to the peasant masses who were living mostly in clay huts and dying of hunger in order to pay their taxes, so they worked to direct their anger against the Jews.

This, then, is our thesis: From 1866 to 1919, anti-Semitism was a genuine state institution in Romania, the basis of its sociopolitical system, propagated from top to bottom by governments aiming at the total ruin of a working population whose misfortune it was not to have had Dacians as ancestors, and to follow the Orthodox Christian religion. This anti-Semitism also turned violent, coming from an ancient anti-Jewish tradition, and to this was added the frustration of certain groups of Romanian craftsmen and businessmen and the position of certain Jews as the most visible agents for the exploitation of the peasants. This latter aspect of the matter is all the more regrettable as the great majority of the peasants, like the great majority of the Jews, shared the same fate of suffering and misery, the former beneath the whip of the boyars, and the latter beneath the sword of the laws and discriminatory regulations.

Can it be said that anti-Semitism was endemic among the mass of the people? Despite the negative stereotype of the Jew shaped by Orthodox theology and a certain literature called "folklore," our answer is negative. Even during times of the most savage expulsions from the countryside, we find many examples of peasants giving asylum to the Jews, even at the risk of prosecution by the judicial authorities. It seems that for generations there had arisen a *modus vivendi* between them and the Jews. But once anti-Semitism became official policy, they were not the last to join in and at the time of the peasant revolts, the Jews were the first to suffer from their pent-up resentment.

It is a paradox that after the Congress of Berlin (1878), which proclaimed the equality of all inhabitants regardless of religious belief, animosity against the Jews doubled in intensity. Public school teachers and university professors were the core of the first anti-Semitic associations, but soon the spectrum enlarged, embracing members of all social classes. Anti-Semitic ideology grew especially through certain literary clubs, but was an integral part of the general ideology of the nationalist movement. Their slogan is well known: "The Jews are a misfortune for us." In that context, anti-Semitic organizations acted as shock troops, with their brutal persecution of Jews; they were used by various political parties, but their political role is almost unimportant. In fact, the parties which shared power after 1866 - the Liberals and the Conservatives - rivaled each other in their zeal for persecuting the Jews by all "legal" means. Not only did most of the press insult the Jews, but even Parliament became a forum from which the deputies gave free vent to invectives against the "Jewish invasion," the "village leeches," this "social disease," against those who represented "a nation within the nation," a "State within the State," etc.

In the second half of the nineteenth century, anti-Semitism appeared in Romania in a most systematic manner through an ingenious series of laws aimed at eliminating the Jews. This resulted in massive emigration. Why was this anti-Semitism more coherent and more active than in most countries?

Was it due to the demographic increase of the Jewish population between 1859 and 1899, which was greater than that of the Romanian Christian population? In 1899 there were 5,925,900 inhabitants in Romania of whom 269,016 were Jews. The latter represented about 4.5% of the total population, 10.5% of the population of Moldavia and about 1.8% of the population of Wallachia. In 1859, those proportions were, respectively, 3%, 9% and 0.4%; the total number of Jews was approximately 135,000. After 1899, after emigration and the natural movement of the Jewish population, a decrease began. In 1912, the number of Jews reached 239,967, or 3.3% of the total population.

Without underestimating the importance of the growth in the number of Jews, this biological presentation of the facts fails to recognize the real foundations of anti-Semitism. This is, in fact, a false problem, for this phenomenon was as deeply rooted in areas with a strong Jewish concentration as in areas where their numbers were low or almost nonexistent (e.g., the countryside). Besides, at the end of the nineteenth century there was already an anti-Semitism without Jews which existed strongly in Western Europe. The answer to the intensity of the anti-Semitic movement in Romania may be sought in the convergence of several factors which we have mentioned and within the framework of a young nationalist state whose anti-Semitism was stirred up by Russia.

A final word before concluding this general overview: in spite of persecutions, in spite of oppressive laws, the Jews of Romania were able to create an original Jewish culture. Paradoxically, government policy, which prevented their integration, retained the ancient structures of the small Jewish community, the *shtetl*, and in spite of poverty and a misery which was often pathetic, the Jews enjoyed a very rich spiritual life. Let us mention in this regard that the Yiddish theatre was born in Romania. It is not surprising that, facing the denial of assimilation and the growth of anti-Semitism, the only possible solution lay with Jewish nationalism. In Romania the idea of Jewish nationalism arose from a traditional Jewish society which embraced a rudimentary nationalism symbolized by the famous phrase "next year in Jerusalem" and developed in the conditions of socio-economic and political crisis which characterized the situation of the Jews at the end of the nineteenth century and the beginning of the twentieth.

To commence our study, we must elucidate the situation of Romania prior to 1866 and the official origin of the Jewish problem which was the root of a virulent anti-Semitism that developed gradually and of which one of the most spectacular results was the departure of nearly a third of the Jewish community.

CHAPTER ONE

DESTINY OF THE JEWS BEFORE 1866

1. Geopolitical Development of Romania

"Eight million people are knocking with entreaty at the door of our Occidental societies. What do they want? They are asking us to help in their rebirth; they seek our alliance. Almost unknown, lost at the far end of Europe, they tell us that they have been buried and cut off from the rest of the human race by long centuries of slavery, neglect, pillage and everything men can suffer." This was how the historian Edgar Quinet began his book on the Romanians in an opening chapter symbolically entitled "A Nationality Discovered."

It was in 1856, at the close of the Crimean War, when the Romanian principalities requested the support of the Western powers in their national rebirth, after "long centuries of slavery." That support was given with alacrity through various treaties and agreements and ten years later, in 1866, when the German Prince Carol of Hohenzollern-Sigmaringen arrived as the head of the country, he found an autonomous and unified Romania. The Ottoman Empire, "the sick man of Europe," still exercised sovereignty, but it was a sovereignty which was all the weaker as the United Principalities of Moldavia and Wallachia stood under the protection of the Great Powers. A first constitution was intended to confirm the new political status of the country and give it a place among the European nations. Adopted under special conditions which we shall discuss later, it provided in Article 7 that non-Christians could not be naturalized. That article was the starting point for legal and methodical discrimination against the Jews living in the country. We must properly inquire what was the status of the Jews prior to 1866 and what was the impact of this new constitution on the Jewish community as a whole. Before taking up the situation of the Jews, it seems useful for us to sketch out the political evolution of the Romanian state. Such a sketch is necessary to reach a psychological understanding of a people "cut off from the human race and having suffered depredations" who, having once obtained a national rebirth, persisted, at the instigation of extremist leaders, to persecute a minority by hastening its marginalization though the constitution and a mass of laws and circulars.

By the conquest of Dacia, Emperor Trajan not only enlarged his empire, but also recorded in the annals of history the birth of a new people, the Romanians. The Romanized Dacians, from whom they derived, maintained a social life with patriarchal institutions after the departure of the Romans and throughout the long centuries of invasion by migrating peoples. At the end of that period, on the political map of the Europe of the thirteenth century, the Romanian nation was separated into three regions: Transylvania to the north and west of the Carpathian mountains; Wallachia, south of the Carpathians as far as the Danube River; Moldavia, to the east between the chain of the eastern Carpathians and the Dniester river. For six centuries, each of those three areas developed in its own way. Whereas Transylvania was incorporated into the Kingdom of Hungary (eleventh and thirteenth centuries), Moldavia and Wallachia evolved quite differently, leading independent lives. The establishment of the Principality of Wallachia goes back to the thirteenth century and the beginning of the fourteenth, when several political regions or voivodates were joined together under the power of a local prince. Present-day Romanian historians consider Basarab I as the founder of the principality. The Principality of Moldavia was established a few decades later but, unlike Wallachia, began with the arrival of a prince from the other side of the Carpathians, first Dragos, and then Bogdan, who united the already existing political structures under their power.

After a period of independence, and facing the irresistible rise of Ottoman power, the Voivod Mircea the Old, voluntarily accepted Turkish suzerainty after his victory over Bajezet at Rovine. A century later, guided by a similar policy of prudence, the Voivod Bogdan of Moldavia likewise agreed to his country's vassalage. How could he have acted otherwise before so powerful an enemy who was then at the apogee of his career? It was Suleyman The Magnificent, who had made the Ottoman Empire the first nation of Europe and western Asia, who, a few years later, personally led his seventh campaign into Moldavia against the Voivod Petru Rares and his inclination towards independence. This resulted in the occupation of Jassy (1538) and the flight of the Moldavian leader, who later changed his mind and was again accepted as the sultan. Thus, through the shrewd policies of Prince Mircea the Old and Prince Bogdan, who accepted the principle of vassalage, the Wallachian and

Moldavian principalities were not transformed into *pashaliks* as were the Balkan countries and Hungary.

In the beginning, relations between the two Romanian principalities and the Porte were those of an external vassalage. It took the form of an annual tribute and the requirement of following a foreign policy in accord with the Sultan's interests. Whereas along the Danube and the Dniester the Turks established fortifications, the principalities were governed by native princes from national dynasties.

Michael the Brave (Mihai Viteazul), who reigned Wallachia from 1593 to 1601, was the most illustrious representative of Romanian national aspirations. First, he obtained independence from Wallachia (1595) and then brought about its political unification with Transylvania and Moldavia (1599-1600). That political and military confederation of the three Romanian regions became a symbol for the Romanian struggle for independence and unity. The situation of the principalities of Wallachia and Moldavia changed at the beginning of the eighteenth century when the Turks imposed a humiliating government on them: they were governed for a century by Greek princes from the Phanar, the Greek quarter of Istanbul. Their task was to exact the maximum economic output from the region and to resist Russian and Austrian influence. The Phanariot regime was imposed because the Porte was afraid of losing its domination over that part of Europe. The battles of Zenta (1697) and the Treaty of Carlowitz (1699) had confirmed the decadence of the Ottoman Empire.

The Phanariot period began in the two principalities with the reign of a single prince, Nicolae Mavrocordatos. He was placed at the head of Moldavia in 1711, replacing Dimitrie Cantemir, who had fled to the Russians after the Russo-Turkish War, and in 1716 of Wallachia, replacing Stefan Cantacuzino, who had been killed by the Turks. The Phanariot century weighed heavily not only on the political growth but also on all other facets of life in the Romanian countries. It ended with the revolt of Tudor Vladimirescu in 1821. The Porte then allowed the appointment of local princes, Grigore Ion Ghica in Wallachia and Ionita Sandu Sturdza in Moldavia.

During the Phanariot period two rich areas were occupied by foreigners. Bukovina and Bessarabia, which had been part of the principality of Moldavia since its creation, were annexed respectively by the Austrians in 1774 and by the Russians in 1812. In view of the decadence of the Sublime Porte, the Russian and Austrian Empires vied for the total annihilation of the Danubian principalities. The Russo-Turkish War of 1828 and the Treaty of Andrinople which followed it in 1829 gave the Russians an excellent opportunity to occupy them militarily for five years and to impose a protectorate on them, while leaving them nominally under Turkish sovereignty. After their departure in 1834 came the period of the princes who governed under the Organic Law. Invested at Constantinople, they were, in fact, subjects of the Tsar.

The revolutionary movement in Moldavia and the Revolution of 1848 in Wallachia had a pronounced nationalist tone and were aimed especially against the Russian Protectorate. But the Russian and Turkish armies occupied the principalities, crushed the revolution and the Romanian patriots were forced into exile. By the Convention of Balta-Liman (1849), the two rival powers restored the *status quo ante* and appointed the princes for a period of seven years (Barbu Stirbei in Wallachia and Grigore Ghica in Moldavia). The Crimean War again brought about the occupation of the principalities, first by the Russian armies (1853-1854) and then by the Austrian and Turkish armies (1854-1856) through the Convention of Boiadgi-Kioï of 14 June 1854. The situation of the Danubian principalities changed under the Treaty and Convention of Paris (respectively, 1856 and 1858). The Russian Protectorate came to an end and the principalities were placed under the guarantee of the Great Powers. The union of Moldavia and Wallachia occurred in 1859, when the *divans ad hoc*, or national assemblies, provided for by the Convention of Paris for the two regions, selected the same prince, Alexandru Ioan Cuza. The latter, through a series of economic, institutional and cultural reforms, endeavored to give the new state a modern character. But Prince Cuza's liberal policies, such as the secularization of Church properties and the abolition of feudal servitude on the large estates, displeased the boyars, who forced him to abdicate in 1866.

The new provisional government offered the crown of Romania to Prince Carol of Hohenzollern-Sigmaringen, who accepted it and made his triumphal entry into Bucharest on 10 May 1866. That election encountered numerous obstacles not only from Turkey, which was displeased by this reinforcement of the new Romanian state and its desire for independence, but also from certain Western powers. In France, Drouyn de Lhuys, the Minister of

Foreign Affairs, looked upon Prince Carol's acceptance of the Romanian crown as an insult to the Conference of Paris. The latter had included representatives of the sponsoring powers and Turkey and had asked the Bucharest government to proceed according to the Treaty of Paris (1856) to elect a native prince and it had been noted that no foreign prince should be placed on the Romanian throne. Finally, Napoleon III, who was the most enthusiastic supported of the union of the principalities on the international scene and who had assisted Cuza, approved the election of Prince Carol, who was related to the French Emperor through his mother Josephine.

Such, in brief, was the geopolitical history of the Romanian principalities which ended in the creation of an autonomous Romanian state at the mouth of the Danube and with a foreign prince of the Hohenzollern family at its head. But by the last third of the nineteenth century, more than half of the territory and population of Romania were located outside the boundaries of the new country. From then on, the struggle of the Romanian nationalists was oriented towards legitimate demands: the return of the annexed provinces to the "mother country" (Transylvania, Bukovina, Bessarabia). The Romanians of the principalities who, as late as the beginning of the last century had a Greek clergy under the Patriarch of Constantinople and a Slavic alphabet dating from the time of Methodius, had never forgotten their Latin origin.

A new intellectual elite which had come primarily from the circles of small landowners and which had been educated in western universities, particularly in France, had introduced into the country the liberal ideas of the French Revolution. This group had taken upon itself the task of gaining recognition for the Romanian nation. Its members came from the most dynamic elements of the Revolution of 1848, of the struggle for union and for independence. The reforms of Alexandru Ion Cuza fell into the same perspective of national rebirth. However, just prior to 1866, Romania was a preeminently agrarian country in which most of the land belonged to a minority of wealthy boyars, whereas the peasants, who had just recently been liberated from serfdom and who formed the mass of the population, lived in outdated conditions and expected other urgent reforms. The new Romanian bourgeoisie began to play an active part in politics. At the time of Cuza, that social class rose slowly but surely and became more and more impatient.

When Prince Carol arrived, Romania stood at a turning point in her history. In that new conjuncture, what would be the place allotted to the Jews? But first, let us see what their situation was before 1866, what were their origins, what was their role and how they were looked upon in the principalities.

2. Origin of the Jews and Their Situation Under the Native Princes

The origins of the Jews go back to the earliest times of Romanian history. There are documents which attest to their presence in Roman Dacia. After the Roman conquest, many Jews came to join those who were already in the country. In Roman Dacia, there were Jews at Sarmisegetuza, the capital of Decebal, at Apulum (Alba Iulia), Ampellum (Zlatna), Tibiscum (near Caransebes). In the reign of Septimius Severus, a Jew named Herrenius Gemelinus was procurator of equestrian rank at Dacia Apulensis, with residence at Sarmisegetuza. At Tibiscum there was an important landowner named Aurelius Secundinus, the son of a Roman knight named Marcus Aurelius Secundus.

Septimius Severus and Caracalla freed the Jews from the oath of allegiance when they came to occupy public office because of their religion. That privilege remained in force in the Roman Empire until the end of the fifth century. So we find Jews in administrative and military positions.

Coins have been discovered in Bessarabia in the area of Hotin, bearing the effigy of Jehuda Maccabeus (second century). Certain Latin inscriptions collected in the *Corpus inscriptionum latinarum* of Theodor Mommsen refer to the Jewish religion and the God of Israel, who often appears under the name of *Deus Æternus*. The presence of Jews in other parts of Roman Dacia (Scythia Minor, particularly Dobrogea) has been proven by epigraphic documents in Hebrew. Under Theodosius I, the prefects were ordered to calm the anti-Jewish movement in the year 379 A.D. and to see that the synagogues and the homes of Jews were respected.

There is lack of evidence concerning the long and troubled period of the mass migrations that affected the Romanian territory in the fifth and until the tenth centuries A.D. relative to the Jews. That is why we cannot speak with certitude, as some Jewish writers tried to do towards the end of the nineteenth century, of genuine continuity between the Jewish presence in Roman Dacia and that of the medieval Jewish communities that existed at the time the Wallachian and Moldavian states were established (between the thirteenth and fourteenth centuries).

Between the eighth and ninth centuries, the Khazars, a people of Turkish origin who had adopted Judaism, extended their empire from the region of the Volga, between the Caspian Sea and the Black Sea, and penetrated into Romanian territory. Some historians have advanced the hypothesis that the Romanian Jews are partly descended from those Khazars.

Although the problem of the Khazar Jews has not yet been explained for lack of precise documentation, there are testimonials to the establishment of Jews in the principality of Wallachia shortly after its creation. Expelled from Hungary by Louis the Great, they arrived there in 1367. That first immigration was well received by Vladislav Basarab and his successors Radu II and Dan I, who granted them privileges in order to encourage trade. Thus, other kinds of Jews were added to the native ones through immigration from neighboring countries. Following their expulsion from Spain in 1492, the Jews spread out over the Mediterranean basin as far as Romania. Documents from that period mention their appearance in Wallachia as early as 1496.

Whereas the immigration into Wallachia was composed mainly of Sephardic Jews in the beginning, in Moldavia it was Ashkenazi Jews who came from Galicia and Poland.

Vlad Tepes, called Draculea, Prince of Wallachia (1456-1462 and 1476), treated the Jewish merchants harshly. At the same time, they were treated better in Moldavia by Stephen the Great (1457-1504). At the latter's court there was a Jew named Isaac Beg, who had come as an emissary of King Uzun Hazan to Moldavia to arrange an eventual alliance between Moldavia and Persia against the Turks. In the city of Bucharest we find the first documented mention of the Jews in the reign of Mircea Ciobanul in 1550. In Moldavia, Petre Schiopul (1578-1579 and 1582-1591) expelled the Jewish merchants who had come from Poland. Following that prince's reign, in 1591, an exceptional event appears to have taken place: for a few months the throne of the principality was occupied by a Jew named Emmanuel. But the sixteenth century ended in tragedy with massacres of Jews both in Wallachia and Moldavia. In November, 1593, the Jewish merchants of Bucharest were massacred on orders

of Mihai Viteazul (Michael the Brave) who found that a good way to
pay his debts to them. Prince Aron the Terrible did the same to
nineteen Jews of Turkish origin.

The number of documents relative to Jews in the first half of
the seventeenth century is rather high, indicating both their part in
the economy and their numerical size. The princes' first appeals are
from this period. In 1612 Stefan Tomsa and Gheorghe Ghica in 1658
invited Polish, Armenian and Jewish merchants from Lvov
(Lemberg) to move to Moldavia.

From the viewpoint of our study, this same period is especially
significant. In fact, we find here the first wave of official, written
anti-Judaism. The first codes of Church canon law appeared during
the reign of Matei Basarab (1634-1654) in Wallachia and Vasile
Lupu (1634-1653) in Moldavia. They contain articles pertaining to
the Jews and the anti-Judaism one finds therein is of classic Christian
inspiration. Matei Basarab published two codes: *Pravila Bisericeasca*
(the Church Code), also called the Little Code, printed at the Govora
monastery in 1640 and *Indreptarea Legei* (Amendment of the Laws),
printed at Targoviste in 1652. The first one, translated from the
Slavonic language by a monk named Michel Mazalie, is a collection
of Church laws providing sanctions against those who do not abide
by the norms of the Church. The second, translated from Greek by
Daniel Panoneanul, is both a collection of ecclesiastical and secular
laws. Vasile Lupu's Code is entitled *Pravilele Imparatesti* (Imperial
Codes) and was printed at the Trei Ierarhi monastery at Jassy in
1646. This collection, translated from Greek by Eustache Biv Vel
Logofat, contains items of canon, penal and civil law. Here we have
legislation of medieval type which is in many ways comparable to
that which long existed in the West. Everyone who did not embrace
the Orthodox Christian religion was considered to be lapsed or a
heretic and was subjected to special treatment. Christians were
expressly prohibited from having contact with Jews. The usual
punishment was excommunication.

The testimony of a Jew was not accepted in courts, except for
that of physicians. That exception was due to Dr. Cohen, the personal
physician of Prince Vasile Lupu, who also acted as diplomatic agent
between the Ottoman Porte and the King of Sweden. For the same
crimes and misdemeanors committed, the punishment of the Jew and
the Christian was generally the same.

We may conclude by stating that the discriminations against the Jews, as well as the regulations concerning them, contained in these legal codes issued solely from religious concerns. The separation of Christians from Jews (and other heathens) was part of a conservative movement within the Church which occurred in other countries and at other times.

The middle of the seventeenth century suffered from the great revolt of the Cossacks led by Bogdan Chmielnicki (1593-1657) against the Poles. That revolt and the events which took place between 1648 and 1658 cost the lives of more than 100,000 Jews. Many Jews were incarcerated in the towers of Jassy and tortured to death. The second half of that century was relatively calm and saw the creation of community institutions which flourished during the Phanariot period. The Jewish communities in the towns and country-side were headed by provosts under a High Provost. Considered to be a corporation like that of the Armenians, the Jews were subjected to taxation. The last native prince, Dimitrie Cantemir (1693 and 1710-1711) gives a portrait of the religious life of the Jews at the end of the seventeenth and beginning of the eighteenth centuries in his monumental work "Descriptio Moldaviae."

3. The Phanariot Regime and the Jews

A new community institution appeared under the Phanariot regime: the *hahambasa*, the spiritual leader of the Jews in the entire country, appointed by a decree of the prince. The first *hahambasa*, Betalel Cohen, the son of Rabbi Naftali Cohen, the Sultan's protégé, was appointed in 1719. That institution lasted more than a century and disappeared in 1834. The *hahambasa* resided at Jassy but the Jews of Wallachia were also under his jurisdiction; he enjoyed certain privileges (tax exemption) like the upper classes. His representatives, called *vekil hahambasa*, were located in the major cities.

During the Phanariot century, the Jewish communities and their institutions were consolidated. Besides the *hahambasa*, there was also the *staroste*, called *roš medina* in Hebrew, at the head of the thirty-three guilds representing national minorities like the Armenians or the Greeks and the different trade corporations. The principal role of the guild was to see to collection of the collective tax imposed on the Jews for kosher meat. An edict of Prince Alexandre Ipsilanti dated 1775 describes the rights and the part played by the *staroste*: he was exempted from certain taxes imposed by the Treasury and acted as judge in deciding quarrels among the Jews. When the sentence was not appropriate or the lawsuit was too important, the prince's Treasurer made the decision. That edict also tells us that the princes themselves took part in the appointment of *starosti*, as they did for the *hahambasa*.

The increase in the number of Jews throughout and especially towards the end of the Phanariot century was due to immigration started and encouraged by the princes of Moldavia, since the principality was under-populated. The new arrivals were asked to create small towns (*targuri*) or to resettle in certain cities or villages. The most urgent calls for immigration occurred at the time of Grigore Ghica in 1736 and 1737 and in that of Constantin Mavrocordat in 1742.

In general, the creation of a new town (*targ*) took place after an agreement had been made between the boyars and the Jews. A decree by the prince confirmed the agreement which granted some privileges. These included land required for the synagogue, the cemetery and a reduction in taxes in the early years.

According to the historian E. Schwartzfeld, the first town founded by the Jews was Onitcani in Bessarabia at the close of the seventeenth century. Their number increased in the second half of the eighteenth century and the last small town founded by the Jews was Dranceni in 1862 on property belonging to Mihail Kogalniceanu.

By the end of the Phanariot period, Jews had spread over all Moldavia and into many parts of Wallachia. They fell into three categories:

- Autochthonous Jews of origin similar to that of the indigenous Romanian element;
- Chrysobulite Jews or *hrisoveliti*, established in the principalities at a more recent date, but gradually melting into the mass of indigenous Jews;
- Subject Jews (*suditi*), under the protection of a foreign power. These were a minority, coming from among the two former groups. They generally chose such protection to escape the fiscal or legal strictures of government bureaucrats. They joined other categories of the population who enjoyed the status of "subjects," such as Armenians, Russians, Greeks and even autochthonous Romanians. Such status derived from an old tradition of the Ottoman

Empire, bestowing a sort of extra-territoriality such as that given to consulates and their staff. The number of such persons increased regularly after consulates were opened in the principalities by Russia (1782), Austria (1783), France (1784) and England (1802). The first codes of civil law were promulgated at the end of the nineteenth century; they were the codes of Ion Caragea in Wallachia and of Scarlat Calimachi in Moldavia. The Caragean Code contains no articles concerning the Jews, but it stresses in general the right of foreigners to enjoy all civil rights, and thus *a fortiori* that of native Jews. The Calimachi Code permitted Jews to purchase houses and shops in the cities, but forbade them from buying rural property.

From the viewpoint of legislation, we can state that, except for certain exceptions, the Phanariot era did not put too many obstacles in the life and traditional areas of activity of the Jewish population, i.e., trade and handicrafts. Nevertheless, there was important discrimination in penal law, in that Jews could not testify against Christians. This stemmed from the earlier codification of imperial laws published by Andronache Donici in 1814. It was used in Moldavia, because the Calimachi Code was not translated from Greek into Romanian until 1833.

The Phanariot regime brought a new aspect of medieval anti-Judaism: accusations of ritual murder. Previously unknown, it took root in the Romanian principalities at the beginning of the eighteenth century. It became so widespread that certain princes tried to stop it. For example, Constantin Ipsilanti asked the Orthodox Metropolitan to explain to the people that there was no basis for belief in ritual murder. This was without success and it continued to the middle of the nineteenth century.

At the same time, a voluminous anti-Jewish literature, encouraged by the clergy and printed in monasteries, was disseminated throughout the principalities. In 1803 there appeared a violent pamphlet written by Neofit, a former rabbi converted to Christianity who had become a monk. One of its favorite subjects was the accusation of ritual murder. The book had enormous success and came out in ten editions. The last was - surprisingly - in 1929! The Jews suffered severely during the revolt of Tudor Vladimirescu in 1821.

But in spite of these occurrences, most Jews enjoyed the real status of natives. That came from a decree by Prince Caradgea in 1817. Article 47 of the Calimachi Code stated that disparity of religion had no influence over the attainment or exercise of rights. But the situation of the Jewish community which had, at the time of the Phanariot rule, received the official name of "Jewish Corporation" - *Breasla Jidovilor* in Moldavia, and *Breasla Evreilor* in Wallachia - changed profoundly after the promulgation of the Organic Laws.

4. The Organic Law and the Beginnings of Legal Anti-Semitism

The Treaty of Andrinople (1829) ended the Russo-Turkish War and marked a period of Russian domination over the Romanian principalities which endured until the end of the Crimean War. Although the sovereignty of the Ottoman Porte was maintained, it was now the representatives of the Tsar who managed the affairs of the Romanian countries. At the beginning of the military occupation, the Russian governor, General Pavel Kisselev, imposed new legislation contained in two regulations which were called "organic" because they set down the basic norms for the internal organization of the principalities. Drawn up in 1830, they went into effect in Wallachia on July 1, 1831, and in Moldavia on January 1, 1832. The two laws are almost identical and that is why they are usually referred to as the Organic Law. Under those laws, it was decided that the reigning prince was to be chosen for life by an "extraordinary national assembly" of 132 deputies (190 in Wallachia), 27 of whom represented the merchants and the craftsmen and the rest represented the boyars. The peasants were not represented. A "National Assembly," a kind of parliament, was composed only of boyars and the higher clergy. It was that Assembly which was to promulgate the law. All of that organization was directly inspired by the autocratic Russian regime. In fact, major influence in the state was attributed to the boyars who took the interests of the peasants upon themselves; it is not surprising that the condition of the latter deteriorated.

Measures in the Organic Law relative to the Jews were generally inspired by the most antiquated views current in the Tsarist Empire. During the reign of Nicolas I (1825-1855) a series of severe restrictions was imposed on the Jews (they were prohibited from living at fewer than 50 *verstes* from the border; the jurisdiction of the rabbis was eliminated, etc.). So the representatives of the most anti-Semitic country of Europe inflicted special and discriminatory treatment also on the Jews of the principalities. By the laws they changed from natives to foreigners, forming a separate nation, deprived of rights. Article 94 of Chapter III in the Organic Law of Moldavia is the most significant. It introduced a new aspect of the matter which had not existed before: that of the vagabond Jew, who could be expelled as being a dangerous element in the country:

> ...It is undeniable that the Jews who have spread into Moldavia and whose numbers are increasing every day are, for the most part, living at the expense of the natives and are exploiting nearly all the resources to the detriment of industrial progress and public prosperity. To prevent this difficulty as far as possible, the same commission will note in the census report the situation of every Jew, so that those who have no status and who are living without authorization, without engaging in any useful occupation, may be removed and that such persons may no longer enter Moldavia.

This article may be the key to the real problem of the Jews which developed tragically after 1866.

The Jews were looked upon altogether as foreigners and were denounced by law (!) as exploiters of the resources of the country and as a retrograde group opposed to economic progress.

The Organic Law proclaimed the principle of belonging to the Christian faith as a condition for receiving civil and political rights. Many discriminatory measures were taken regarding the Jews. For example, Article L in the chapter "Concerning the Jewish Community" prohibited Jews from farming land for the first time.

The military occupation of the principalities ended in 1834, but Russia remained the protecting power. In Moldavia, Mihai Sturdza (1834-1849), Alexandru Ghica (1834-1842) and Georghe Bibescu (1841-1848) in Wallachia, carried on this anti-Jewish policy introduced by the Organic Law. The era of the Protectorate opened the way for bribery (*bakshish*) in the corrupt government. Thus, certain regulations concerning the Jews could be avoided by the wealthy.

The Organic Law and a number of later laws also changed the structure of the Jewish communities in the principalities. The law no longer allowed the Jewish community the title of "Corporation of Jews," but rather of "Jewish nation." The autonomy of the old corporation disappeared from a fiscal and legal point of view and now there was a progressive integration of the Jewish population within the general administrative framework. The supervisory positions of *hahambasa* and *staroste* disappeared and were replaced by new ones whose election and authority were determined by government decision. The spiritual leader, the great rabbi, was no longer appointed by the prince, but elected by the Jews and, in losing the title of *hahambasa*, he lost the rights pertaining to that position. The *staroste* was replaced by a commission of ten persons elected to represent the community.

Whereas the changes in community organization were almost identical in Wallachia and Moldavia, the demographic development was quite different. There was a considerable increase in the Jewish population of Moldavia from the beginning of the century due to immigration from Bessarabia following its seizure in 1812 and also to a high birth rate. In 1803 there were 30,000 Jews in Moldavia, in 1848 about 60,000, and the census of 1859 brought them to 118,922. In Wallachia, in 1838 there were 5,960 and in 1860, 9,234 Jews.

Under the new organization, the Jewish communities obtained legal status which allowed the authorities to intervene to apply decisions under the new laws (these decisions had both a religious and community character, since the right of judgment had been transferred to the country courts). But at the same time the government acquired an almost absolute control over community affairs, which was used particularly to increase the taxes.

Growth in the number of Jews in Moldavia through immigration which had been encouraged by Prince Mihai Sturdza for the purpose of creating new settlements, or of increasing the population of others, was in contradiction to the laws on vagrancy which allowed the authorities to expel even native Jews from the country. In fact, this was only an apparent contradiction, for the real purpose of those laws was not to stop immigration, but to extract the most money possible from the Jews. The various decrees on vagrancy, some promulgated and some rescinded, were invoked as a pretext for the systematic persecutions carried out after 1866. During the time of the Russian Protectorate, using Tsarist legislation as a model, the

Jews were prohibited from settling in the villages, from leasing property or setting up industrial firms in the cities. These regulations seemed to be inadequate in the eyes of certain parts of the population and several petitions were sent to Mihai Sturdza which demonstrate the virulence of the annoyance felt towards the Jews, who were denounced as usurers and monopolizers of trade and the professions. Representatives of the new Christian middle-class, fearing the economic competition of the Jews, asked that immigration be halted and called for many discriminatory regulations. Religious resentment was still alive and the book *Prastia* ("Sling"), published during Sturdza's reign, is a masterpiece of traditional attacks against the Jews.

The important characteristics of development in the Jewish communities during this period of "regulation" were the following: considerable demographic increase and the growing role of the Jews in crafts, business and banking; adaptation of the community structures to the requirements of the Treasury, and restrictive laws which tended to consider all Jews as foreigners, thus encroaching upon the rights of native Jews and shutting them away from public affairs.

Although the Organic Law was introduced into the principalities by the Russians, they must not be held solely responsible for the growth of legal oppression. The great landowners felt a foreboding and fear that their immense holdings would soon be divided up and so they had an interest in keeping the Jews in an inferior position, using them always as scapegoats for the inhuman life of the peasants. This is why they worked to have anti-Jewish legislation expanded.

In the view of the historian Nicolae Iorga, the Organic Law was based on the will of the boyars:

"The Organic Law," he wrote, "was largely based on the draft constitution drawn up by our boyars, particularly those of Moldavia, and placed the Jews among foreigners whom only the National Assembly could naturalize for special merit."

The generous feeling of tolerance of the revolutionaries of 1848 was quite the opposite of those uncompromising attitudes.

5. 1848: Illusive Promises

The "springtime of nations" also came to the Danubian principalities and the Revolution of 1848 can be looked upon as "a repetition in miniature of the European revolutionary movement as a whole," as David Thomson wrote in his book, *Europe Since Napoleon*. It bore a national stamp through its struggle against the Russian Protectorate and also against Turkish sovereignty and it had a social side expressed in many reforms that it demanded.

The revolutionary movement started first in Moldavia, but it failed before reaching any real proportion, so that it cannot be called a genuine revolution, but only an attempt at one. It took the form of riots in the town of Jassy and the presentation of a petition to Prince Mihai Sturdza for the purpose of improving the economic and political situation of the country. The demands made in the petition were rather moderate (school reform, creation of a national bank and a discount bank, tenure for the public officials) and only a few such as the abolition of censorship, the establishment of a National Guard, the dissolution of an illegally elected Chamber and the right of appeal to the Public Assembly were in contradiction to the Organic Law. To gain time, the prince pretended to accept the petition, but during the night of 28-29 March 1848 he had the leaders of the movement arrested and then expelled them. Among those deported to the other side of the Danube was Alexandru Cuza, the future prince. Enjoying Russia's unconditional support, Mihai Sturdza was soon able to announce the end of the rebellion. In August, 1848, Mihail Kogalniceanu, who had taken refuge in Bukovina, published the program of the Moldavian revolutionaries *"Dorintel partidei nationale in Moldova"* (Aims of the National Party in Moldavia). The demands were expressed in thirty-six articles of which these were the principal ones: autonomy of the country, equality of civic and political rights, a National Assembly made up of representatives of all social classes, freedom of the press, abolition of the death penalty, freedom of religion, nationalization of the property of the convents, abolition of slavery, the union of Moldavia and Wallachia and the emancipation of the Jews.

Although it was published several months after the disturbances in Jassy and at a time when the revolution no longer had any chance for success, by proclaiming for the first time equality of civic and political rights and the emancipation of the Jews, the program of the revolutionaries marks an important date in the history of the Jews in Moldavia.

In Wallachia the revolution was better prepared by the nucleus of Young Wallachs, including a group called *Dreptate, Fratie* (Justice, Brotherhood). Its leaders were recruited from among young intellectuals returning from France, where they had seen the February Revolution, or from patriotic writers, such as Nicolae Balcescu, the brothers Ion and Dimitrie Bratianu, C.A. Rossetti, Ion Ghica, Ion Eliade Golescu, and others, from among anti-Russian boyars like the wealthy and influential Golescu brothers, and from ambitious military men like Gheorghe Magheru and Christian Tell. The revolutionaries succeeded in forcing Prince Gheorghe Bibescu to abdicate and held power for three months, from June 11 until September 13, 1848. One of the first acts of the provisional government was the Proclamation of Islaz, taken from the name of the place where the rising had begun on June 9. It contained twenty-two articles for a new constitution. Article 21 decreed the emancipation of the Jews and political rights for all compatriots of other religions. This article began to take effect when a Jewish banker, Hillel Manoach, was appointed member of the Bucharest City Council.

How did the Jews react to these events? The Jews only took part in the Revolution of 1848 on an individual basis, which was perhaps due to the fact that there was no forum in the principalities which represented all of the Jewish population.

C.A. Rossetti, as Minister of the Interior, spoke thus of the part played by the Jews: "As far as payment is concerned, the Jews have paid me by taking my hand in a brotherly way when I was in exile on foreign soil; they even paid me with their blood, for, six years ago, one of them gave his life for my country: David Rosenthal."

In our study entitled "The Revolution of 1848 and the Jews in the Danubian Principalities," we came to this conclusion: the participation of the Jewish intellectuals in the revolution was a revealing attempt to break the chains of the ghetto and seek integration in the life of the country, but in contrast with the Western countries where liberal ideologies, radical and even socialist ones replaced the Law of Moses, in the Romanian principalities the revolutionary Jews remained attached to their ancestral Jewish tradition.

For most Jews, especially those of Moldavia, the Revolution of 1848 meant the beginning of a new way in their life. Emancipation received a new impulse of which one of the first signs was the fight for changing the traditional costume (the *caftan* and the *shtramel*). As early as 1847, a group of young Jews requested and obtained from Prince Sturdza a law allowing them to change from the

"Polish" clothing. But the law stirred up a very lively reaction and brought about a split between conservatives and liberals.

As in the case of Moldavia, the revolutionary program could not be carried out in Wallachia, because the attempt at creating a democratic republic ended when the principality was occupied by the Turks. The Russians occupied Moldavia and the two powers restored the Organic Law.

For the Jews, the revolution of 1848 meant illusive promises. But for the first time, in the eyes of Christian society, the Jews no longer appeared as a religious entity excluded from the political business of the country. Under the influence of the liberal ideas of 1848, the condition of the Moldavian Jews who made up the majority of the Jewish population of the principalities improved. During the reign of Prince Grigore Alexandru Ghica, under whom the period of the Organic Law came to an end, several favorable laws were adopted, including: resumption for Jews of the right to purchase vineyards; limitation of the laws on expulsion to Jews of recent immigration; a law on the recruitment of Jews in the Army. However, a decree dated August 5, 1862, according to which Jewish synagogues might not be built within 150 feet from a Christian church, illustrates the persistence of deeply rooted prejudice.

Until 1856, the Jews continued to enjoy certain civic rights, but not political ones. Their situation changed after that date and we shall examine the first Occidental interventions in their favor.

6. The Jews During the Rebirth of the State (1856-1866)

For Romanian patriots, a large number of whom had lived in exile after the repression of the Revolution of 1848, the Crimean War seemed to be an ideal occasion for bringing about the "holy" union of the principalities. Memoranda, brochures, hearings and various other initiatives were used to publicize the national Romanian aspirations. Their theater of operations was in the capital cities of western Europe, especially Paris.

Despite certain hesitations in view of the international political situation at that time, Napoleon III, who had become "the arbiter of Europe" after the Crimean War, became the most enthusiastic supporter of Romanian regeneration, of the creation of a united, autonomous country.

The Emperor's government took its first initiative in favor of a united Romanian state at the Conference of Vienna (March 1, 1855), through his delegate, Baron Bourquenay. He added to his draft memorandum on the union a note suggesting the appointment of a foreign prince. The representatives of England and Austria were opposed to this and the Ottoman Porte categorically refused. The Conference of Vienna ended without any decision relative to the union of the principalities and the subject was entirely ignored at the Conference of Constantinople in January, 1856. But once the question had been raised, it then became a favorite theme in relations between the different powers.

At the Congress of Paris, which began in February, 1856, Count Walewski proposed the union, but due to the systematic hostility of Austria and Turkey, the treaty was signed on March 30, 1856, without solving the problem. However, the decision made in Articles 21-27 changed the international status of the principalities, which were placed under the joint backing of the contracting parties, maintaining the sovereignty of the Porte, but abolishing the Russian Protectorate. The Treaty of Paris called for revision of the Organic Law according to the will of the Romanian people, which was to be expressed in the framework of elected national assemblies called *divans ad hoc* and later approved by the European powers through a new treaty. The *divans ad hoc* of Moldavia and Wallachia agreed on four principles as a basis for the future organization of the principalities. These were as follows: guarantee of the autonomy of the principalities; union of Moldavia and Wallachia into a single state, governed by a single government; choice of a foreign prince; a representative constitutional government.

In spite of these decisions and France's efforts, the Paris Convention of August 19, 1858, did not proclaim union. The Convention stipulated that Moldavia and Wallachia, henceforth called United Principalities, under the sovereignty of the Porte and the guarantee of the Great Powers, would continue to be two separate states (!), with two *hospodars* elected for life, two governments, two assemblies elected for seven years, but a single Supreme Court and a central committee which would draw up the laws for the country. Finally, the Romanians removed the difficulty by electing the same prince, Alexandru Ioan Cuza, to the thrones of both principalities in January-February, 1859.

What was the influence of all these events on the situation of the Jews?

By proclaiming complete freedom of religion, Article 23 of the Treaty of Paris in 1856 which ended the conference which was held in the same city represented progress with respect to the religious restrictions contained in the Organic Law. But the Treaty contains no article concerning equality of civic and political rights, different from the Protocol of the Conference of Constantinople which mentioned it explicitly. The Conference of Paris (1856) preferred to leave the regulation of that question to the *divans ad hoc*. While the Wallachian assembly limited its deliberations to discussion of the four principles mentioned above, the Moldavian assembly expanded debates on the future internal organization and drew up the theory of a Christian state which gave political rights only to Christians. In view of this attitude, the Romanian Jews, supported by Armand Levy, sent petitions to the commission of the protecting nations at its offices in Bucharest. At the same time, they requested help from French members of their faith. Walewski had been alerted to the situation of the Jews, which had not been addressed either by the *divans ad hoc* or by the international commission at Bucharest, and on June 5, 1858, he submitted to the Conference of Paris, which was to approve the decisions of the Romanian assemblies, a model document for the future internal organization of the principalities. That document included the principle of freedom of religion and that of the equality of civic and political rights, as follows:

> The law constituting the organization of the principalities should coordinate all regulations and those relating to all public services, in such a way as to avoid conflicts of authority and at the same to satisfy all the requirements of a government based on the principle of equality, so that the Moldavians and Wallachians may all be equal before the law, with respect to taxation and have equal access to all public offices in each principality without distinction of origin or religion.

Walewski also expressed his support for improvement in the condition of the Romanian Jews in a letter to Baron de Rothschild dated July 24, 1858:

> Monsieur le Baron,
> your son has had a letter sent to me in your name with a petition to the Paris Conference by Jews living in Moldavia. The Emperor's government has always been sympathetic to the cause of religious toleration and the equality of religion before the law and you cannot doubt the interest with which I received your communication. I should be glad if present circumstances allowed me to contribute to improvement of the condition of the Jews in the Principalities.
> Yours sincerely, etc.

But the generous ideas expressed by Walewski, which were part of France's liberal tradition, the government of Napoleon III was not able to introduce into the Paris Convention. Article 46 of that Convention only contained a vague promise of the eventual granting of political rights:

> The Moldavians and Wallachians will all be equal before the law, in taxation, and may have access to public office in each principality.... Moldavians and Wallachians of all Christian confessions will have equal political rights. Enjoyment of those rights may be extended to other religions by legislation....

How can one explain the failure of the French proposal relative to the status of the Jews? It was probably due to the hostility of Russia with whom the Emperor was trying to deal tactfully and with whom he had intended an eventual alliance since 1856. But the deeper cause lay in the opposition of many Romanian politicians who did everything, first in the *divans ad hoc* and later at the Paris Conference, to make a difference of religion a criterion for the granting of political rights.

That discriminatory position of the unionist patriots contrasted sharply with the reaction of the intellectual elite as well as with that of the Jewish population who had strongly supported the "holy" union. From that point of view, it is significant that the first Jewish newspaper in the Romanian language, *Israelitul Roman* (The Romanian Jew), which appeared at Bucharest in 1857, published articles right from the start in favor of the idea of union.

In spite of their desire for integration in the life of the country, in spite of their struggle and foreign support, of which the most important was that of the French government, the Jews of the principalities were not granted political rights at the close of the period of union (1856-1859).

It was only during the reign of Alexandru Ioan Cuza (1859-1866) that the condition of the Jews improved and that the promise contained in Article 46 of the Paris Convention came close to realization.

A new uniform code of law was adopted, replacing the differing ones which continued in the two principalities. Then the legal status of the Jews underwent an important change expressed in Article 26 of the Community Law of May 31, 1864, and in the Civil Code of 1864.

The category of native Jews, called into question at the time of the Organic Law and which represented the majority of the Jewish population, was officially recognized by Article 26 of the law. For the first time, they could take part in municipal elections, provided they fulfilled the following conditions: army service with the rank of noncommissioned officer; study at an institution of higher education or at a Romanian university; receipt of a diploma from a foreign university with the degree of doctor or *licentiate*; had established in Romania a factory "useful to the state" which employed at least 50 workers. Although these laws retained a significant distinction between native Christians and Jews, it is still true that the passage of the community law was a beginning of political emancipation. One result of this was the appointment of a Jew, Adolph Buchner, as Inspector of Finance.

After the coup d'état of 1864, Prince Cuza decided to bring out a new code of civil law. It was promulgated on December 6, 1864, and implemented the following year. Articles 8, 9, and 16 contained measures relative to the status of the Jews. They did not grant full political freedom to the Jews, but naturalization was made possible under certain conditions. In fact, however, no Jew was naturalized prior to Cuza's abdication in February, 1866.

In conclusion, we can say that during Cuza's reign the native Jews enjoyed full civil rights. Even foreign Jews enjoyed them except that they could not buy real estate, which was a privilege reserved for foreigners of Christian faith. Native Jews also experienced the beginning of political emancipation. Prince Cuza outlined his policy to a Jewish delegation which had come to present him New Year's greetings on January 1, 1864, as follows:

> In 1864, the Jews may congratulate themselves on many rights. Before receiving a petition on that subject, we had decided on gradual emancipation, attempting to grant civic and political rights little by little which would be equal to those of other classes. I should have liked to give you everything, but I could not. You will receive gradual emancipation. However, where I have been, I have loved you and I have never made any distinction of a religious nature.

The event which affected the Jewish community life the most was the government decision of July 3, 1862, to no longer supervise the internal organization of the Jewish communities. In appearance, they received greater autonomy, but in fact the communities lost their legal status which had been recognized before. The Jewish population, which had up until then been able to retain the essential traits of its traditional life in spite of the interference of the authorities in their affairs such as internal elections, and worship, welfare, health and education, was now disoriented.

On the religious plane, one of the most spectacular results of the struggle between the modernist current and the traditionalist one was the expulsion in 1864 of Rabbi Malbim at the request of a group of Jews in the capital. This did not bring about the defeat of the traditionalists and although the Jews of Wallachia, through the Spanish community in Bucharest, give us the picture of absolute assimilation, the Jewish masses of Moldavia kept, for a while, their Polish clothing and their Yiddish universe.

It should be pointed out that Dr. Iuliu Baras, one of the founders of Romanian medicine, was the first to start the struggle for the civic and political emancipation of the Jews in Romania through a pamphlet he published in Paris in 1860 called "Jewish Emancipation in Romania." This began the long series of polemics on that subject which reached more than 300 by 1919.

From the socio-economic viewpoint, prior to 1866, the Jewish community of Romania acted in general as a middle-class. The Jews represented the middle-class in the best way. In the Moldavian countryside, it was by cultivating the land and by retail trade. They were the useful and hated intermediaries between the powerful boyars and the peasants. In the cities and towns, many of which had been established by them, the Jews carried on their usual occupations: all types of business, handicrafts and trade.

By changing their status which had been made so precarious by the Organic Law, and by looking upon the Jews as "Romanians of Jewish religion," despite opposition to their emancipation and the enduring hostility of certain elements of the population, the liberal laws of Prince Cuza had rekindled the hope for impending redemption.

CHAPTER TWO

THE JEWISH PROBLEM BECOMES OFFICIAL

1. Article 7 of the Constitution of 1866

The government installed in February 1866 after the forced abdication of Cuza, who was replaced a few months later by a foreign prince from a noble German family, Carol of Hohenzollern-Sigmaringen, began for the Romanian Jews a period filled with harassment and persecution. One of the first steps of the provisional government was to exclude Jewish soldiers from the National Guard. But paradoxically the chances of the Jews to obtain political emancipation and thus total integration into the life of the country had never been as close to realization as in 1866. The occasion for this was the first constitution which was to be promulgated by the national agencies. On the day of his triumphal entry into Bucharest, Prince Carol formed his first government with Lascar Catargiu, head of the Conservative Party, as Prime Minister and Minister of the Interior. The cabinet was composed of five politicians belonging to various wings of the Conservative Party, also known as the "Whites" and of two Liberal ministers, also called the "Reds." The presence in the government of representatives of the liberal movement of 1848 which had called for the emancipation of the Jews, should, in principle, have influenced the Constituent Assembly favorably in solving that problem.

Hoping to obtain equal political rights through the articles of the new constitution, the Jews also called on the Central Committee of the Universal Jewish Alliance in Paris to bring influence to bear on those responsible for Romanian policy in that direction. Contact between the Jews in Romania and the Central Committee of the Alliance had been established shortly after the creation of that body.

Approaches were immediately made to the Romanian government which replied that it would present to the Chamber a draft law granting civic and political rights to all Romanians without religious distinction. In spite of repeated promises from Ion Bratianu and from Balaceanu, chargé d'affaires for the principalities at Paris, because of the hostility of many parliamentarians from Moldavia and the excitement that existed in Bucharest as the promulgation of the constitution drew near, it was decided that Adolphe Crémieux, who was then at Constantinople, would come to Romania. The president of the Universal Jewish Alliance reached Bucharest early in June and was warmly welcomed. In a famous speech before members of the government and fifty parliamentarians, a well-known orator noted that it had been a French Jew (Victor Schoelcher) who abolished Negro slavery in the colonies.

His address impressed the audience favorably and was repeated in the press. The government and the Chamber had apparently accepted the idea of the need for granting equal political rights. Crémieux left Romania persuaded that the cause for which he had fought would be crowned with success. He had also obtained a formal promise from the young Prince Carol, whom he met on June 14, 1866, as follows: "These prejudices are shameful and I shall put my honor at stake to fight them. The complete emancipation of the Jews will have my most active and devoted support."

The government gave Parliament an article favorable to emancipation of the Jews which ran like this: "The status of Romanian is acquired, retained and lost according to the rules established by civil law. Religion cannot be an obstacle to citizenship."

But an important change was added, demanded by the committee responsible for writing the constitution: "Religion cannot be an obstacle to citizenship." This remained as it was. Then the following was added: "As far as the Jews are concerned who were previously established in Romania, a special law will provide for their gradual admission to naturalization."

That new text was a step backward with respect to the Civil Code, as it no longer recognized the possibility for native Jews to be naturalized under the existing civil laws and only declared that a future law would arrange for gradual admission to naturalization. Article 6 was not the final word and the parliamentary session which drew up the laws relating to the Jews met from 18 to 30 June 1866. While the discussions went on in Parliament, an excited crowd came there and demonstrated against the granting of rights to the Jews. The Minister of Finance, Ion Bratianu, under the influence of that "popular" demonstration which had really been organized for that purpose, declared that the government was withdrawing the article relative to the Jews. "Gentlemen," he said, "we have said that the government does not intend to give the country to the Jews nor give them rights which endanger the interests of Romania in any way."

The demonstration quickly changed into an anti-Jewish riot: the large synagogue which had been recently built and was one of the most beautiful buildings in the capital was ransacked and pillaged. Some Jews were mistreated and their houses and shops ruined. After the events of June 18 and 30, 1866, Jews who were foreign subjects sent a petition to the consuls requesting protection and asking the Romanian government for energetic measures to prevent new attacks.

This riot drew a strong reaction in Europe, especially in the countries which, under the Treaty of Paris, acted as guaranteeing powers, but before the protests of the Ministers of Foreign Affairs of France and Great Britain reached Bucharest, the famous Article 7 of the Constitution was adopted which shut off the political emancipation of the Jews for more than half a century. Its text was as follows:

"The status of Romanian is acquired, retained and lost according to the rules established by civil law. *Only foreigners of Christian religion may become Romanians* [italics added]."

That article gives an official color to the Jewish problem in its historical perspective. Foreign Jews could never be naturalized as Romanians. By superseding legislative measures taken earlier by Prince Cuza, the Constitution of 1866 not only raised a barrier against the political emancipation of native Jews, but indirectly placed them in a precarious situation. In the future, they could be (and were) treated as foreigners against whom many discriminatory measures were directed. In order to understand better the later decisions of Minister Ion Bratianu against the Jews, we think it useful to reproduce here a few passages from his address which easily succeeded in convincing a Chamber which was already favorable to reject emancipation:

> The Jews have become a social plague, not because they are more backward than us, for we have a class which is more backward than them, a social stratum lower than the Jews; they are the Tziganes, and we have given them rights without hearing anyone object. Nor shall I raise against the Jews the consideration that they are less civilized, but simply that of their large number which everyone says is a threat to our nationality, and

> when the nation is threatened she defends herself
> and becomes not intolerant but provident. It is
> only by administrative regulation that we can save
> ourselves from this disease and prevent the
> foreign proletariat from invading our country.

Facing such an attitude and after the unfortunate outcome of the article in the Constitution on the Jews, Crémieux wrote on July 28, 1866: "In Romania, the Liberal Party which professes loudly that it holds the most advanced points of view and warmly sympathizes with the Revolution of 1848, this Party, I am forced to say, is still in the fifteenth and sixteenth centuries as far as religious and social questions are concerned."

The profanation of the great synagogue, the adoption of Article 7 of the Constitution and the policy begun by Bratianu in the spring of 1867 caused the Jewish problem to become official throughout Europe.

2. Bratianu's Circulars and the Consequences Thereof

The new oppressive pressure began scarcely three months after the Constitution was voted into law, on September 6, 1866, when the government, after an order from the Minister of Interior, Ion Ghica, decided to reactivate Article 94 of the Organic Law.

That article, as we have seen, made no distinction between native and foreign Jews and its purpose was to expel the Jews for reason of vagrancy. In 1867, the measures taken by Ion Ghica were confirmed and broadened by Ion Bratianu, who had become Minister of the Interior. Through a series of circulars sent to the prefects, he called for energetic steps to get rid of the "vagrants" and decreed that the Jews no longer had the right to reside in rural communities, to operate hotels and cabarets and to lease properties. He asked for these directives, which also involved Jews in the cities under the pretext of the crime of vagrancy, to be strictly carried out.

Unfortunately, this was done. The situation this created for the Moldavian Jews was as follows, according to Castaing, Chancellor of the Consulate of France at Jassy:

Monsieur le Marquis,

...On the pretext of eradicating vagrancy, he [I. Bratianu] has ordered the administrative authorities to expel from the country all Jews who cannot prove that they were engaged in a visible profession or hold certain capital. Unfortunately, there is too large a number of Jews who have come from Galicia and Russia who have no visible means of support and of whom it would be desirable for the country to get rid. But this should have been done in a more regular way, less obvious, and in any case according to the Civil Code which provides that vagrancy be declared in a court sentence. By attributing that right to the police, the Minister violated the law and has caused inevitable abuses of power in a country where venality and arbitrary actions are the distinguishing traits of the population. Right from the start, the subaltern policemen set out to chase the Jews. The Prefecture and the police stations were immediately filled and it has been said, which seems credible to me, that they are only arresting persons who can pay for their freedom, while turning a blind eye on those who deserve expulsion. It is generally held here that M. Bratianu only intended this as a political maneuver. He thought that by supporting the general antipathy of the population of Jassy against the Jews, he would create a diversion from the thoughts of separatism which are being actively fostered by Rosnovano, Letzesco and Aslan, the leaders of the separatist party. But he did not attain that objective and the only result has been to rekindle hatred against the Jews.

The following was included in a letter sent to Crémieux by the Jewish community of Jassy:

...The same Minister marked his recent arrival at
Jassy by a still more barbarous ordinance, order-
ing the police to carry out raids on the Jews under
the pretext of vagrancy and before the Minister's
eyes, the police have been gathering up masses of
Jews for several days, without any control by the
courts, of all classes and ages, using unheard-of
brutality, using force and having them deported
by soldiers to the other side of the Danube. This
sad scene, accompanied by the jeering of the
populace on one hand, and by the cries of distress
of the women and children of our unfortunate
deported colleagues, is being repeated all the time
in the streets of Jassy and is taking on more
threatening dimensions from day to day. Under
such persecution coming from Minister Bratianu
and the agitation of certain party leaders who are
igniting the fanaticism of the people, we are
threatened with general massacre....

That description needs no comment. Let us add that the mayor
of Jassy replied to complaints by a deputation of Jews: "There is
something which is higher than any law, our right as Romanians as
owners of this country to expel you, who are only tenants. So you
must understand that you have to leave the country where that is
your only status."

These activities aroused discontent within Romania itself and
in May, 1867, fourteen politicians, mostly Moldavian boyars, went to
Prince Carol and asked that they be stopped.

The Universal Jewish Alliance carried on a wide campaign in
the news media and with the European governments on what was
happening in Romania. The republican Crémieux obtained an
audience with Napoleon III, who said: "This oppression cannot be
tolerated or understood. I shall tell this to the Prince." Crémieux
replied:

And I, Sire, shall transmit your good words to my
unfortunate colleagues in Romania. They will be
consoled and given hope. If the Emperor

expresses his opinion publicly and the blame he places on these mediaeval barbarities, they will stop and reparation will be made. As for me, I shall turn to the press; I know that its sympathy will help us and that all voices will be raised against this hateful persecution aroused by a Minister of a constitutional government.

Two days later, on May 26, 1867, Emperor Napoleon sent this telegram to Prince Carol:

I cannot leave your Highness unaware of how public opinion is troubled by the persecutions of which it is reported that the Jews have been victim in Moldavia. I can still not believe that the enlightened government of Your Highness is authorizing measures which are so contradictory to humanity and civilization.

The French press and that of the other European countries castigated the action of the Romanian authorities. In *Le Siècle*, Henri Martin called for granting political rights to the Jews. He wrote:

The Jews in Romania are looked upon as foreigners. Thus, in spite of themselves, they are a floating population. Make them citizens! We are not suggesting that this be done unconditionally, but Jews born in Romania should be assimilated to all the other citizens, as well as those who have been there for 30 years (a generation), and those who do not fulfill such conditions should be treated like all other foreigners with respect to naturalization. Certainly this is neither too much nor is it Utopian.

The Central Committee of the Alliance requested and obtained the intervention of the English, Austrian and Italian governments. After receiving reports from their consuls in Moldavia, the different powers protested vigorously the acts of expulsion which were as arbitrary as they were cruel.

The Romanian government published the following reply to all those protests in *Monitorul oficial* of May 26, 1867: "The measures taken against the Jews were simple acts of hygiene and police to which all citizens are subject."

The members of the Central Committee of the Alliance decided to intervene directly with the Romanian authorities and Prince Carol. At the same time as a broad campaign of information and open propaganda aimed at improving the condition of the Romanian Jews, Adolphe Crémieux also encouraged private and secret steps as indicated by his initiatives with the lawyer Émile Picot, Prince Carol's French secretary.

3. Adolphe Crémieux, The Alliance and Émile Picot

Prince Carol was disturbed by the extent of the remonstrances and by the Western press campaign, which openly demanded Bratianu's resignation, so he decided to send his personal secretary to Paris to contact members of the Central Committee of the Jewish Alliance.

Émile Picot was an attorney and a former judge of the Council of State. He had obtained his position in Romania through the protection of Hortense Cornu, a foster sister of Napoleon III who had suggested naming Prince Carol to the throne of Romania. She had written to Prince Carol after Napoleon III had received Crémieux in audience saying that if Bratianu was really devoted to him, he would resign at once. She had also written to Émile Picot in a similar vein.

Picot conferred with the Central Committee of the Alliance, but its members were not pleased with his explanations. They hoped that he could serve as an intermediary in the Jewish question with Prince Carol.

Due to pressure from abroad and particularly, it seems, because of Napoleon III's displeasure, Ion Bratianu resigned on August 16, 1867, followed by the Prime Minister, C.A. Cretulescu, who had already announced his departure three weeks before. Bratianu's withdrawal was only a fiction, for the new cabinet formed on August 29 under Stefan Godescu followed all the directives of the preceding ministry.

Then Crémieux wrote to Picot, informing him that the Alliance had declared a sort of truce for the moment and was refraining from any action which might irritate the Romanians. That truce would soon be broken by new persecutions, but the letter showed a change concerning the Jewish problem in Romania. Crémieux no longer asked for the granting of political rights as he had in 1866 and simply called for a declaration of civic equality. As the ministerial circulars had deprived the Jews of an entire series of civil rights, he realized that he had to face the requirements of the moment. But he did not give up the idea of complete emancipation of his Jewish colleagues in Romania.

Picot summarized the situation as he saw it in a letter to Madame Cornu dated August 26, 1867, as follows:

>...Without mentioning my sojourn in Moldavia and the steps I have taken in Paris, I have continued to work actively on this matter since my return. I have studied the old laws and the modern ones; I have received various letters from M. Crémieux; I had a very long conversation with Sir Montefiore. Well, on this point, they are not listening to me. The Prince, informed by Mr. Bratianu that what he had done was well done, finds that everything is going well and the measures taken by the Ministry which, in their present form, are in complete opposition to the laws of the country, have not been rescinded. What bothers me most is that the Prince, to whom I am sincerely attached, thinks that I am the victim of intrigues directed against him. I only see him for a few moments each day and then for the purely technical part of my work. Friedländer has the master's ear... The change in the Ministry has turned into a feint by which we must not be deceived; in reality, Bratianu is still in control....

In an essay that Picot published after his stay in Romania, he concluded:

>Whenever the Jews see themselves treated without prejudice they will have confidence and will attach themselves to the country which persists in

looking upon them as foreigners. They are not
insisting on obtaining political rights which the
government refuses to give them, but their entire
emancipation should now be the objective of the
Romanian government and we hope that it will be
one day a title to glory for Prince Carol.

4. Sir Moses Montefiore Visits Bucharest

Another attempt to improve the fate of the Romanian Jews and
end their vicissitudes was that made by Sir Moses Montefiore, a
British statesman and philanthropist who devoted much of his life to
helping Jews suffering from persecution. At the age of eighty-three,
he decided to go to Bucharest and ask Prince Carol for a change in
his policy towards the Jews. His trip resonated widely throughout
Europe and prior to his trip, he obtained the support of the governments of Great Britain, France, Austria, Italy, Prussia and Russia, so
that their representatives in Romania would help make his visit a
success.

Marquis de Moustier, the French Minister of Foreign Affairs,
wrote to V. Castaing, the French chargé d'affaires and Consul at
Galatz as follows:

> Sir Moses Montefiore is coming to the Principali-
> ties to make some permanent arrangements with
> the Moldo-Wallachian government in favor of the
> Jews in the Danubian provinces and he has re-
> quested our support in achieving success in this
> humanitarian mission which he has undertaken.
> We can have no doubt concerning the regrettable
> acts of which the Jews have been victim and we
> have already informed Prince Charles of the
> painful impression they have made on the gov-
> ernment of the Emperor. These feelings have
> acquired new strength after the deplorable inci-
> dent which has just taken place at Galatz. I ask
> you to assist the efforts of Sir Moses Montefiore
> within your area of jurisdiction and to stress with
> the agents of the Moldo-Wallachian government
> that they should put a final stop to this persecution

which has resonated in such a disturbing manner
throughout all Europe.

Sir Moses Montefiore arrived in Bucharest on August 22,
1867. He was well received by Prince Carol and was assured that the
situation of the Jews would improve. In a letter he submitted to the
Romanian prince on August 27, 1867, Montefiore stressed that he
had undertaken this trip after having received the support and the
approval of the governments of the guarantor powers. His request
was quite modest: he only asked that the Jews enjoy the protection of
the authorities for the safety of their persons and their property.

Prince Carol replied that their was no religious persecution in
Romania and that he would always see to the protection of the Jews
as to that of all other Romanians. Receiving this promise from
Prince Carol, Montefiore abandoned his planned trip to Moldavia
and upon his return to England published in *The Times* on September 20, a letter concerning the assurances he had received. On that
subject, Castaing, the French Consul at Galatz, reported to his
Ministry new disturbances "which do not agree with the favorable
measures expressed on that occasion to the venerable representative
of the English Parliament and with the hopes which he seems to have
brought from the capital of the United Principalities."

However, his presence in Bucharest brought about malicious
demonstrations and an outburst from the anti-Jewish press. The
periodical *Natiunea* accused the English baronet of having come to
the principalities "to turn them into a new Palestine, to take their
territory and their products away from the Romanians."

During his visit, he also became acquainted with Émile Picot.
Through him and as a sign of goodwill, the Prince sent his portrait
to the great philanthropist. Montefiore expressed his thanks for the
gift and for the reception he had been given.

After his visit, new expulsions were ordered during the month
of September. In October, the same prefect who had been responsible for the drowning of several Jews in June, expelled more than
thirty families from the district of Covorlui. In November, a
confidential circular was sent to the prefects by Stefan Golescu, who
was now Minister of Foreign Affairs, approving those measures. A
month later, the sub-prefect of Bistrita ordered summary expulsions.

During this period, the government denied any trace of
oppression. In a letter of December 21, 1867, E. Cretulescu, the

Romanian chargé d'affaires at Paris, excused himself for being unable to take part in the General Assembly of the Alliance and noted that "the present situation of the Jews in Romania is entirely satisfactory." It was quite the opposite and, from 1868 up to the Congress of Berlin, there was a series of actions which resulted in the constant intervention not only of Jewish organizations but also of the Great Powers.

CHAPTER THREE

PERSECUTIONS AND INTERVENTIONS: 1868-1877

1. The Disturbances of 1868 and the Draft Law of the Thirty-One and the Great Powers

On January 6, 1868, a violent anti-Jewish riot broke out at Barlad in Moldavia. It started after the death of a priest named Varnav, who had come to the city as an official candidate to the Chamber of Deputies (to which he was elected). In order to obtain a maximum number of votes, he had made virulent speeches against the Jews. The population accused the latter of having poisoned him. While the police observed nothing, the mob, with axes and other weapons, attacked Jewish homes and shops, led by a law clerk and a professor.

After Sir Moses Montefiore had sent a letter to the Romanian Prince, calling his attention to the excesses which had taken place at Barlad, the Romanian Minister of Foreign Affairs, Stefan Golescu, while deploring the clash, threw the responsibility onto the Jews, saying: "...the truth compels me to add that, according to the results of the inquiry which is underway, it was your colleagues who unfortunately caused or provoked the incident."

While expulsions were taking place at Padurea lunga and at Galatz, the city walls were covered with placards reading thus: "Christians, arise! The time has come to kill the Jews, the Freemasons and their friends. God is with us!"

All these disturbances again brought about the intervention of the Jewish Alliance, which send an urgent appeal to the Great Powers to help the Romanian Jews.

On February 22, 1868, Bismarck replied to the Central Committee of the Alliance that his representative at Bucharest had received an order "to use all his influence to guarantee the Jews the protection which is due to them in all countries whose laws are based on the principles of humanity and civilization."

The policy of the authorities did not change and on February 22, other expulsions were ordered by the prefect of Vaslui. At the beginning of the month of March, they continued in the district of Bacau. Here is an example of a notification of expulsion:

Romania   March 8, 1868

To Mr. Mendel sin Ouscher

Mr. Mendel,
     I, the undersigned mayor of the Commune of
Beresti, in view of the many orders of the government and the many which have been given you
to leave this commune, and considering that you
have not followed these orders, I am setting a
final and unimpeachable limit of ten days, after
which I shall be forced to take the necessary
measures.

The Mayor
(Illegible signature)

     On March 12, 1868, Adolphe Crémieux wrote to the French
Foreign Ministry:

> ...Ask for the prosecution of the rioters and the
> looters in the courts which will punish their
> crimes, the dismissal of that prefect and that
> mayor, who are bringing blame on the govern-
> ment, the abolition of the exceptional regulations
> against the Jews, the reparation due to the families
> of the victims and to those who survived the
> persecution of which they were the object, this,
> Monsieur le Ministre, is what we are asking of
> you. Certainly France has the right to speak
> strongly to that government which owes it its
> creation and its legal existence. Your voice will
> certainly be listened to.

     Before the French government had had time to intervene,
another event upset the facts of the Jewish problem in Romania. On
March 24, 1868, thirty-one of the radical Moldavian deputies calling
themselves *Fractiunea liberala si independenta* (Liberal and Independent Fraction) filed a draft law placing Jews outside common law.
All Jewish committees were to be dissolved; the Jews were forbidden

from living outside the cities, owning buildings, leasing land, taking part in public sales, forming partnerships with Christians, engaging in any trade or industry without holding an authorization which could be revoked at the pleasure of the government. It was called a "Draft Law to Regularize the Situation of the Jews in Romania."

Article 1 - Jews may not reside in urban communes without the authorization of the communal councils. They may not reside in rural communes under any pretext, even temporarily.

Article 2 - Jews guilty of infringement on the preceding Article will be considered vagrants.

Article 3 - Jews may not own real estate either in the cities or in the country. The sale and purchase of any real estate in favor of a Jew is legally null and two-thirds of the price will be given to local welfare institutions; the other third will go to the informer.

Article 4 - Any individual who had collaborated in the violation of the preceding measures will lose his political rights for from 3 to 10 years and will pay a fine of 20% of the value of the purchased property.

Article 5 - No Jew may rent land, cabarets, mills, distilleries, bridges, vineyards, stables for raising cattle, pastures, sheepfolds, inns or hotels on the main highways. Likewise, they may not be entrepreneurs for any government business, or that of the communes or of any public institution.

Article 6 - Government officials are prohibited from processing any request from a Jew regarding partnerships or other business which contravenes the dispositions contained in Article 5.

Article 7 - For a Jew to engage in any business or trade, he must hold a special authorization paper issued by the authorities of the commune where he has chosen to live. Anyone failing to do this will be fined from 50 to 300 francs. Officials may not process a claim from a Jew who does not hold this authorization.

Article 8 - Any business relative to foodstuffs or beverages for Christians is prohibited for Jews. However, they may sell these wares to their co-religionists. Any infraction of this prohibition will entail a fine of 100 to 600 francs. In case of repetition, the authorization paper will be withdrawn.

Article 9 - All Jewish communities and committees which have been allowed up to now in the different towns are, and remain, abolished when the present law is published.

Article 10 - All laws, ordinances, decrees and regulations contrary to the present law are, and remain, abrogated from the day of its publication.

This draft law provoked an immediate and unanimous reaction in the Occident. On March 26, 1868, the Marquis de Mostier asked Boyard, the French representative at Bucharest, for explanations of the draft. The latter replied on April 6 to the Cabinet, but he said that it was nevertheless "the consequence of the ferment which the government has allowed to grow for a year against the Jews."

On March 29, Delaporte, the French Consul at Jassy, wrote his impressions to the Ministry of Foreign Affairs as follows:

> Recently a meeting was called at the municipal City Hall by a deputy from the Red Party who had come from Bucharest expressly to report on a draft law presented to the Chamber against the Jews, and, at the same time, to obtain a petition signed by the residents of Jassy supporting this law.
>
> The promoters of the draft law are a group of teachers at the Barnoutz school who have, since last year, made persecution of the Jews an essential condition for their support of Minister Bratianu. This group, which includes about 15 members of the Chamber, recruited, in order to present this draft law, a large number of deputies who belong to Mr. Bratianu's personal party and support the present Ministry without condition or reservations. So it is well known and incontestable that the persecution of the Jews is the work of the government itself. The Ministry is using it to gain popularity with the masses, or better said, the voters in those cities where there are only people who have been fanatacized against the Jews.
>
> The motive for this persecution cannot be attributed alone to the obsolete ideas of some and the immorality of others. The speculative turn of mind and the activity of the Jews, and the traditional fault of the Romanians to seek public office as their only career, a fault which removed them

from the commercial and industrial professions which they despise and scorn, have resulted in most of the small industries, particularly in Moldavia, as well as all of the domestic and foreign trade, falling almost exclusively into the hands of the Jews. Besides, all of the country's banks belong to Jews. Up to now the Romanians have not only shown little aptitude for financial business, but they are not highly regarded either as businessmen or industrialists. Consequently, the nation's capital is preferably placed in the hands of Jews and no deal can be made without them. Hence, with some there is a feeling of envy and animosity which is hardly justifiable from a moral point of view, and with others there is a fear which may be sincere although with little basis of seeing the Jews establish real power in Romania. Thus one aimed at the poorest and most miserable section of the Jews when the real target was the wealthy merchants. Now they want to deny them all civil rights, in order to succeed in expelling them from the country and ruining them. This regrettable tendency is quite clear in the new draft law presented to the deputies.

Crémieux contacted the representatives of the Great Powers in Paris, who assured him of the support of their governments.

In England, Sir Francis Goldsmid addressed the Cabinet in the House of Commons and Lord Stanley answered that the government was very worried by the matter. He said: "I think this is a matter that affects the Christians more directly than the Jews, for although the suffering falls on them, the dishonor falls upon the Christians."

Even before the vote of the Chamber in Romania was known, the government officials began to apply the draft law as though it had been passed. In the Bacau district, the prefect Lecca ordered the expulsion of 500 families within twenty-four hours.

At Movileni, the mayor, N. Gheorghe, ordered the Jews to leave the commune within twenty-four hours and there were other expulsions. At Bacau, the National Guard was called in to protect citizens' homes, but attacked the Jews, firing on their homes, profaning the cemetery and desecrating the graves.

These acts brought lively protests from the foreign representatives in Bucharest. The government denied the facts, but an inquiry made on the spot by the efforts of the consuls of France, England, Austria, Greece, Prussia and Russia at Jassy proved their veracity. On April 15, 1868, they made a joint protest to Stefan Golescu, the head of the government, which ended thus: "Consequently, the undersigned have been led regretfully to the conviction that the categorical denials given the agents and Consuls General of Bucharest by the Romanian government are in flagrant contradiction with the facts which they have been in a position to confirm."

The government persisted in its denials which provoked the reaction of Baron von Eder, Austrian agent and Consul General, who denounced the prefect of Bacau and asked for indemnification of the victims.

Facing the stern remonstrances of the Great Powers, Prince Carol had the guilty prefect removed and reshaped his Ministry on May 11, 1868. The new head of the government was Nicolae Golescu, the brother of his predecessor. A new attempt was made to have the draft of the Thirty-One adopted in the form of a law referring to trade unions, but it was withdrawn on June 6 and the Jews could again take part in property sales by auction, as provided by a ministerial circular.

In the same year there was a terrible riot at Galatz which illustrates the extent of popular resentment against the Jews, one of whom was accused of having tried to extract the blood of a Christian child. Jewish houses were vandalized and pillaged; ninety persons were injured.

Castaing reported this and described the looting of the synagogue:

> ...Other scenes of violence and devastation took
> place almost at the same time as in the Jewish
> quarter. The synagogue was invaded by a mass of
> rioters who broke doors and windows and entered
> inside. There, nothing escaped their destructive,
> looting rage. All the objects of worship, the holy
> books and the candelabra were removed and torn
> up or broken to bits. The chests were forced open

and the money they contained disappeared. In the vicinity of the school, several houses were destroyed, among them that of a person under French protection who operated a small school at his own expense which had likewise been sacked by the rioters. I intend to have the losses listed and the damage as far as possible by the local authorities....

Following the riot, the Committee of the Jewish Alliance at Bucharest sent an urgent petition to Prince Carol. This time there was a prompt reaction, for the prefect of police was fired and the Jews were paid damages through the insistence of Baron von Eder.

The new Ministry headed by Dimitrie Ghica was formed on November 28, 1868, and declared in a statement to the parliament on December 2 that it opposed the bullying of the Jews, but that it would not allow Romania to be "entirely populated by Jewish colonies."

The next year the repression doubled in intensity.

2. The Circulars of Kogalniceanu and Their Consequences

In 1869 it was the Minister Mihail Kogalniceanu, the former patriot of 1848 who wrote Article 27 of the Program of the National Party of Moldavia on the political emancipation of the Jews, who took up the policy of expulsions from the countryside which had been carried out so well by Bratianu.

For that liberal of 1848, eviction had become a useful means for attracting the new middle class to his cause. The Jews for whom he had demanded emancipation twenty years earlier had become "the scourge of the countryside."

In a single year he sent out eight circulars which brought the intended results: Jews were expelled, mistreated, robbed. The number of those expelled from the districts of Roman, Vaslui, Tutova and Covorlui alone came to more than 1,200 men, women, and children.

On December 21, 1869, Kogalniceanu declared proudly to an anti-Semitic Deputy named Codrescu: "According to everything he (Bratianu) says , I believe that as Minister of the Interior I have done much more than he or anyone of you; yes, gentlemen, I have ordered everything a minister could order; I have cleared the villages of the Jews by every means."

Again, the Jewish Alliance intervened against his expulsions.

Barons Alphonse and Gustave de Rothschild and Adolphe Frank spoke with Prince Carol who came to visit Paris in the fall of 1869. Previously, the French government had sent a note on June 15 through the French Consul General at Bucharest Mellinet to the Ministry of Foreign Affairs of Romania expressing the hope that the circulars would be withdrawn.

Kogalniceanu answered by a violent note, saying that the Jews were foreigners, outside the law, and for the first time, instead of denying the persecutions, he revolted against this interference in the internal affairs of his country. Thus the idea was launched and henceforth all of the governments were to repeat that leitmotiv: the Jewish problem was a Romanian problem, an internal one, and no country had the right to intervene.

The anti-Jewish campaign carried on by the government, resulted in criticism by the Great Powers and, on the other hand, that of the parliament, which considered the measures taken against the Jews as too moderate. Minister Kogalniceanu replied that he was prepared to enforce all the laws which might be voted against the Jews.

This dangerous turn in the Jewish question aroused the concern of the Great Powers. England took the initiative in calling for a collective diplomatic intervention, but although France and Austria agreed to the English proposal, a collective approach to the Romanian government could not be made because of the opposition of Germany, which claimed that such a step would constitute serious interference in the internal affairs of Romania.

The Romanian government ended by giving the Great Powers partial satisfaction through a circular sent to the prefects which Prince Carol presented as a revocation of Kogalniceanu's circulars. The expulsions stopped, but a number of riots broke out during the same year, causing violence with the usual succession of ransacked homes, looted synagogues and injured people. The year 1871 was relatively calm for the Jews, but after 1872, under Ion Ghica, other events poisoned the social climate.

3. Riots and Discriminatory Laws

A riot that aroused worldwide interest broke out on January 24, 1872, at Ismail, which started with a robbery committed by a Jew who had been baptized in the cathedral of that city. The scene was described by the Jewish community for the benefit of their co-religionists in the West as follows:

> Dear brothers:
> The pen falls from our hands and our heart sinks at the thought of the misfortunes which have fallen upon us: the picture is terrible! It recalls the Inquisition and the Saint Bartholomew's Day massacres. The masses ran like wild beasts escaping from their cage, urged on by intriguers and fanatacized by priests, through the streets, crazy with revenge, rape and murder. They ran from house to house, heartless and without pity, not sparing anyone because of age or sex, not even nursing children. Powerless to remain, our brothers were shamefully mistreated; women and girls were raped in front of their husbands and fathers; our homes were sacked, our sacred objects destroyed, even the rest of the dead was disturbed and the tombs looted; many died from the mistreatment; many women and girls are hiding their shame on straw pallets; a mass of people have no clothing; sick people nowhere to go....

Similar scenes of looting took place at Cahul on January 30 and at Vilcov on February 2. These acts of violence had a wide effect on public opinion in the West. On February 4 the foreign consuls sent a collective note to the Ministry of Foreign Affairs calling for protection of the Jews. The Minister answered by a circular note dated February 19 that the government had energetically put a stop to the disorders, but shortly afterwards a jury at Buzau acquitted the instigators of the rioting and severely punished a number of Jews, including the rabbi of Ismail, who were entirely innocent of having taken part in the theft. This verdict caused indignation and the Consuls General of Great Britain, France, Germany, Austria-

Hungary, the United States and Greece protested in a collective note dated April 18. Expressing their surprise at the decision of the Court of Assizes of Buzau, they declared that the double verdict "indicated the danger to which the Jews remain exposed in Romania." That is why "the governments of the undersigned will have to determine if the impunity granted to the attackers of the Jews will not encourage the return of violent scenes which are unworthy of a civilized country which, as such, should guarantee freedom and security to all religious groups."

The Ministry replied in a circular sent to its representatives abroad in which the Jews were accused of being responsible for the outbreaks. However, it stated that of the six Jews condemned, the government had pardoned two and had commuted the punishment of three others; only the one who had committed the robbery would suffer the entire penalty.

These events gave rise to parliamentary debates in England, Italy, the United States and Germany from April to September 1872; for the first time, in addition to the powers which had guaranteed the stability of the principalities in Europe, the United States expressed its disquietude over the situation of the Jews in Romania. Mr. Washburn, the American Minister in Paris, asked M. de Remusat, the French Minister of Foreign Affairs, for France to intervene. He replied that the position of the Jews was in danger, saying that "the passions of the population and the weakness of the authorities had placed the lives of the Jews in danger and also the security of their establishments." As had often been the case in the past, he said that he would not neglect any opportunity to bring about "equal protection in Romania for all religious beliefs."

The disturbances and expulsions stopped for a while, but the government continued to pursue its anti-Jewish policy through legislation. The law on the sale of tobacco dated February 6, 1872, provided that "the employees of the business as well as the tobacco sellers must be Romanians." On April 14, 1873, a law was passed concerning liquors in which Article 8 read as follows: "In the rural communities, the sellers of alcoholic liquors may not obtain the necessary license unless they are included on one of the lists of registered voters in a rural community." The Jews did not have that right and a number of families were ruined when that law was expanded to include isolated inns located on the highways. As in most of the restrictive laws, the name of the Jews did not even appear for they were considered to be foreigners.

There was a quick reaction from the West and the British government took the initiative to propose a joint intervention at Bucharest. The French Minister of Foreign Affairs, the Duke de Broglie, replied first, saying that "there could only be one point of view when it came to recommending to the government of the Prince the feelings of tolerance and humanity which alone can pave the way in that region for the principle of equality before the law."

The Italian Minister of Foreign Affairs, Visconti-Venosta, indicated his agreement. The German government only expressed its thanks for the invitation and the Austrian government did not answer. Russia refused categorically. Prince Gortchakov sent a memorandum in which he stated that the new law could be considered from three points of view: ethics, form and law. From the ethical point of view, he said that Russia could not disapprove of "a government which seeks to build a wall to protect the population of the villages from a pernicious element which is trying to corrupt the working class and exploits their labor." As to the form, there could be no objection, for "by presenting a law the Chamber of Deputies at Bucharest had spared the sensibilities of the Jewish people, as the law was not directed against them. Only indirectly, as voters. Thus they were spared the open humiliation of a law intended exclusively against their co-religionists." From the standpoint of law, the Treaty of Paris recognized and guaranteed "the rights which the Romanians possessed *ab antiquo.*"

The Romanian Minister of Foreign Affairs Boerescu replied to the Powers that Article 22 of the Treaty of Paris did not allow them to interfere individually in the affairs of the principalities.

England's initiative failed, but Boerescu, mindful of his country's reputation in the West, promised that Article 8 of the aforementioned law would be annulled, but the parliament refused to do so.

In 1875, the government headed by Lascar Catargiu succeeded in inserting the principle of discrimination against the Jews into a document of international law, namely a trade agreement with Austria-Hungary. It provided that Austrian Jews would be treated in Romania in the same way and under the same laws as Romanian Jews. It was criticized in the Austrian Parliament and also in Hungary, but the desire of the Austrian government to install itself in

Romania was stronger than the cause of its Jewish subjects and the treaty was signed. Following Austria's example, Russia signed a commercial treaty with Romania which contained the same discriminations regarding the Jews.

On the other hand, England, France and Italy refused to sign that kind of agreement and only agreed to a provisional trade treaty. The *Gazetta d'Italia* wrote on November 19, 1876:

> The question remains open and six months from now, when this purely mercantile and temporary agreement ends, either Romania will have accepted the principle of the absolute equality of religious (*perfetta egualianza degl'Italiani in Rumania senza distinzioni di culto*) or else it will have no treaties with us and besides it will have placed itself outside the community of nations.

It may be noted that the attitude in France was the most intransigent and ten years later, in 1885, it still refused to sign a commercial treaty with Romania.

The disagreement among the Great Powers was made quite clear and the Romanian government could pass laws against the Jews as it wished.

In 1876 a law was passed allowing the Jews to enter the army, but since an earlier law of 1874 stipulated that "no one may be appointed second lieutenant unless he is Romanian or a naturalized Romanian," the Jews could not attain that rank. Other laws excluded them from being head surgeons in departments and arrondissements.

In conclusion, the prohibitions against the Jews prior to 1877 were as follows: they could not reside permanently in the countryside and could be expelled from there as vagrants by administrative decree; they could not own houses, land, vineyards or any buildings in the countryside; they could not lease land; they could no operate hotels, cabarets or any liquor store in the countryside; they could not sell tobacco; their right to own houses or buildings in the cities was constantly questioned; they could not take part in any public adjudication; they could not be teachers, attorneys, pharmacists, government physicians, or railroad employees; they were subject to military service, but could not reach the grade of second lieutenant;

and the trade treaty with Austria proved that Romania intended to apply its property laws even to Jews of foreign nationality.

To complete the picture of the Jew prior to the Russo-Turkish War, we must mention the new campaign of expulsions in 1876 and the riot at Darabani in June, 1877. The expulsions took place particularly in the region of Vaslui under the prefect Nero Lupascu, the brother of the prefect concerned in the drownings at Galatz. More than 800 persons were involved and were handled with much harshness, according to the statements of some of those expelled. Many of those expelled were generously aided with temporary shelter by peasants who treated them with consideration, even requesting the authorities not to expel certain persons whose character they guaranteed.

As usual, the Romanian government denied the evictions at first. However, in a letter to the Austro-Hungarian consul, prefect Lupascu did not deny them and as some of those expelled were Austrian nationals, the question was brought before the parliament at Vienna. Later, the British State Secretary Bourke made a bitter criticism of the Romanian government before the House of Commons. Finally, three sub-prefects were removed and Lupascu resigned. He was soon after elected to the House of Deputies.

As before, riots soon followed the expulsions. The most serious was at Darabani on June 9, 1877, where all the houses in the town, which was entirely Jewish, were attacked, looted and destroyed by peasants from the vicinity. The Jews were beaten, injured and one was killed. The following investigation dragged on for a long time and finally all the rioters were acquitted.

During this period, what were the reactions of Jewish leaders and organizations in the West?

4. Benjamin Peixotto's Mission

After the visits of Adolphe Crémieux and Moses Montefiore to Bucharest, another Jewish personality, moved by the oppression which continued in spite of official denials, decided to share the fate of his co-religionists of Romania. This was Benjamin Franklin Peixotto (1834-1890) who, after having studied law, wrote editorials for the *Cleveland Plain Dealer* and held various positions of responsibility in American Jewish organizations (in particular as President of the Independent Order B'nai B'rith from 1863 to 1864). He was appointed Consul of the United States to Romania, where he arrived in January, 1871. Peixotto received that post as a result of the intervention of Joseph Seligman (1819-1880), a famous businessman, with President Grant, who was one of his friends. The President agreed to open the first American consulate in the Romanian capital after having been assured that its budget would be covered by several Jewish organizations, the most important of which were B'nai B'rith, the Board of Delegates of American Israelites and the American Romanian Society, of which Joseph Seligman was president. A few influential Europeans also contributed to the financial requirements of the consulate.

Peixotto's mission to Romania was unique in diplomatic history because he was appointed Consul of the United States, a purely honorary position, for the sole purpose of improving the situation of the Jews; President Grant wrote in his letter of credentials that Peixotto was appointed for "missionary work for the benefit of the people he represents."

Peixotto himself looked upon his mission as an overriding duty to change the life of the Jews in Romania and according to him, the best way was by education. He wrote to his friend Simon Wolf in San Francisco: "...The many poor Jews must be assisted with money and counsel.... Schools must be planted throughout Romania and modern education...introduced.... The salvation of the people of Israel, in all countries where despotism rules, lies in the emancipation from their superstitions, forms and ceremonies of the past...."

Shortly after his arrival at Bucharest, Benjamin Peixotto founded a weekly review in German, the *Rumänische Post*, beginning on April 16, 1871. This publication was to be a forum for his ideas for improving the condition of his co-religionists. Visiting Moldavia and seeing the miserable situation of the Jews, he understood the great effort which still had to be made to improve it. To do this, he counted on the support of all the Jewish organizations, including the Universal Israelite Alliance, whose help he requested in an eloquent letter to Adolphe Crémieux. It showed his inner desire to create an organized action which would be more effective in helping the Romanian Jews. It was due to the combined efforts of the Jews of different countries that substantive help was brought to the unfortunate ones. After bloody riots in southern Bessarabia at Ismail, Cahul and Vilcov, Peixotto wrote on July 27, 1872, to the Central Committee of the Alliance:

You will undoubtedly be glad to hear that through the combined efforts of our brethren in London, Berlin, Vienna, Mannheim, Mainz, Pest, Worms and Bonn, as well as your contributions and those of London which were first to arrive, I was able to distribute nearly 40,000 francs to our unfortunate brothers.... I also want to emphasize the noble cooperation throughout all this by Sir Francis H. Goldsmid; the Romanian Jews owe him a debt for which they can never be sufficiently grateful. We have put all Europe and America in movement to help our oppressed brothers and we must not let the movement stop, but continue to work without slackening.

But Peixotto did not stop with signing the collective protest of the Consuls General at Bucharest or with asking Prince Carol to pardon the Jews who had been unjustly sentenced by the jury at Buzau. He also turned to the Jewish communities and urged them to defend themselves. He said: "Everyone must do this for himself and the whole nation; it will increase respect for the Jews by their enemies and prevent attacks on those whom they thought unable to defend themselves."

Being a man of action, and seeing that the Romanian authorities were unwilling to improve the condition of the Jews, Peixotto circulated the idea of mass emigration to America. But that did not coincide with the views of the Israelite Alliance, whose committee at Bucharest declared that it did not approve his project.

On the other hand, many committees were formed in America to encourage the Jews' departure and the Romanian press devoted much space to this proposal. Certain newspapers even suggested that facilities should be made available so that the country might be freed "of its greatest scourge."

Most of the Romanian newspapers, while calling for emigration, presented the matter this way: If the Jews emigrate, they are not patriots, hence they did not deserve to have rights; if they do not emigrate, that is the best proof that they are not being persecuted and thus all the accusations in the international press are lies.

History has shown that Peixotto was right, for, during the great wave of emigration at the end of the nineteenth century and beginning of the twentieth, nearly one third of the Jewish community left Romania.

The situation of the Romanian Jews was taken up by all the large Jewish organizations in the West and committees were formed in many places to help them. In Berlin, the president of the Romanian Committee was a banker named Gerson Bleichröder. With the consent of the local committee of the Alliance, he launched the idea, which echoed that of Peixotto, of a Jewish conference with members from various countries, to discuss ways to improve the condition of their co-religionists in Romania and in other Balkan countries. Held at Brussels on 29 and 30 October 1872, it was the first Jewish "summit" of modern times. The record of the conference declared that "this meeting is striking proof that all Israelites without distinction of nationality are united by the same feeling of solidarity."

Crémieux was the president, while Sir Francis Goldsmid of London, Professor Moritz Lazarus of Berlin and Dr. Leopold Rompert of Vienna, were vice-presidents. Thirty delegates took part, representing the Jews of France, England, Germany, Belgium, Holland and Romania. They made two important decisions: to encourage sending a petition from the Romanian Jews to the Chamber of Deputies calling for equality in civic and political rights, a suggestion made by the Romanian representatives, and the creation of an executive commission in Vienna for the purpose of propagating educational and moral reforms among the Romanian Jews. That commission was to include representatives of the Alliance committees and special committees to be set up to help the Romanian Jews.

The emigration project was disapproved in energetic terms as follows:

> The conference has unanimously rejected any thought of emigration from the soil of Romania. That idea is looked upon as criminal by Romanian Jews whose devotion to their country has been shown in all the deliberations of the conference; such a decision would cast suspicion on the justice of Romanian Christians who are the brothers of the Romanian Jews and whose cooperation they must have to ensure the destiny of their common nation.

The petition of the Romanian Jews was postponed and finally was not brought up for consideration

Following the Brussels conference, there was an organized and energetic international reaction. A memorandum was presented to the Italian Minister of Foreign Affairs on 1 April 1873 by I. Costa and R. Ascolia of Leghorn, who received them and assured them that the Italian government would continue to use its influence to bring about more tolerance from the Romanian government.

In Vienna, a deputation from the Jewish Alliance presented a memorandum to the Minister of Foreign Affairs, Count Gyula Andrássy, concerning the law on the sale of alcoholic liquors.

In England, Sir Francis Goldsmid proposed inviting all of the European and American committees to join in a declaration of protest against the Romanian violation of international treaties.

As for Crémieux, he continued his discreet correspondence with leading Romanian politicians like Boerescu, who promised the eventual and gradual emancipation of the Jews. But there was no sequel to his promise.

Crémieux also contacted the Duke Decazes, the French Minister of Foreign Affairs, but later wrote to Isidore Loeb, the Secretary of the Alliance, that he did not have much hope for action by the Minister, since the French government had no influence in Bucharest. Weakened by its defeat in the Franco-Prussian War, France could not only play a secondary role in Romania, where the foreign policy of Prince Carol had changed drastically after the battle of Sedan, Germany was now added to the traditional powers which counted in the Principalities, namely Turkey, Russia and Austria.

Jewish solidarity became apparent in a striking way in 1876 at the end of the war which Turkey wages against Serbia and Montenegro which had joined to support the insurrection in Bosnia and Herzegovina. The Conference of Constantinople was intended to end that war and deal with the fate of the Christian population of the Balkans. It was a good opportunity for also raising the question of the Jews and, in order to submit concrete proposals to the conference, the Israelite Alliance, at the suggestion of the Anglo-Jewish Association, called an important meeting. The second Jewish conference was held from 11 to 15 December 1876 in the consistorial hall of the temple in rue de la Victoire, which had been made available by the Paris Consistory. Presided over by Crémieux, the participants included members of the Central Committee of the Alliance, various French Jewish leaders and delegates from Germany, England, Austria, Belgium, the United States of America, France, Italy, Switzerland and Turkey.

The conference decided to send a memorandum to the governments of Germany, England, Austria-Hungary, France, Italy and Turkey and a copy was given to Prince Orlov, the Russian ambassador in Paris. The memorandum outlined the precarious situation of the Romanian Jews and contained two demands: to grant complete civic, political and religious equality to all non-Muslims in the provinces of Turkey with which the conference was to deal, and in the Principality of Serbia; and to revise and extend the Paris Convention of 1858 with respect to the Jews in such a way as to guarantee them full enjoyment of civic and political rights.

Charles Netter, a member of the Central Committee of the Alliance, received the mission to go to Constantinople and to make contact with the plenipotentiaries sitting at the conference.

This memorandum was well received by the different governments, but the Jewish question could not be arranged because the conference failed when Turkey refused to accept the Russian demands. War between the two rivals soon broke out again. In fact, according to Salomon Fernandez, the correspondent for the Alliance at Constantinople, the situation of the Jews was not even taken up, in spite of the efforts of Charles Netter with the Grand Vizir Midhat Pasha and the Ottoman Minister of Foreign Affairs, Safvet Pasha.

This attitude may be explained by the fact that the position of the Jews was looked upon as secondary to the many political questions to be solved by the Constantinople conference which finally ended in failure. But at the same time it apparently confirmed that most of the initiatives made by the Great Powers to the Romanian government were of a purely formal nature. Their political or economic interests took precedence for many over the principles of justice regarding the Jews.

In 1876 Peixotto's mission came to an end. The American Consul had not succeeded in his initial task and the Romanian Jews still lacked political rights and many civic ones. His project for mass emigration could not materialize either at that time, since the Romanian government refused to grant the 15 million francs suggested by him for that purpose. However, his mission had not failed for, through his many activities he had awakened a feeling of national dignity among his co-religionists and the hope of redemption.

The Russo-Turkish War of 1877, in which Romania took part, found the Jews of that country in a precarious situation.

At the Congress of Berlin which followed in 1878, the fate of the Jews of Romania and of the other Balkan countries, which had been timidly raised at the Constantinople conference, held a central place in the debates. The Congress marked a new phase which was paradoxically tragic in the history of the Romanian Jews. Before presenting its impact on the Jewish situation and the new outbreak of anti-Semitism, we believe it necessary to analyze the causes which made that phenomenon so violent during the years from 1866 to 1877.

CHAPTER FOUR

FACTORS IN THE
RISE OF ANTI-SEMITISM

The liberal measures taken by Prince Alexandru Ioan Cuza had strengthened hope for a complete integration of Jews in the life of the country and for an end to the Jewish problem which had arisen from the Organic Laws. But the new Hohenzollern regime, during the first ten years, instead of continuing the liberal policies of Cuza, institutionalized the Jewish problem by Article 7 of the constitution of 1866 and by a policy of systematic oppression. What new factors impelled the same persons who had demanded in 1848 equal political rights for their "Jewish brothers" to support persecution?

What were the causes for this change? How can one explain the rise of anti-Semitism which took on such violent aspects at that time as are shown by the expulsions and the mass rioting? It cannot be denied that the root of the evil must first be sought in the religious tensions which never ceased to exist and became more serious after 1866. Despite official denials, the persecutions certainly involved this facet of the matter.

1. The Religious Factor

With Article 7 of the Constitution decreeing that only foreigners of Christian faith might acquire Romanian citizenship, religious discrimination became official. This discrimination was also shown by laws and administrative measures which were as arbitrary as they were numerous.

For example, in 1867 the town of Galatz prevented the rebuilding of a synagogue which had been destroyed during a riot, within less than 150 yards of a church. In the same year, at Roman, the mayor prevented the construction of the traditional boots (*soukot*) for the Feast of Tabernacles, using a fire prevention ordinance as a pretext. At Barlad, an attempt was made to prohibit the ritual slaughtering of animals under kosher rules. In 1869, the mayor of Roman placed an excessive tax on kosher meat. But most humiliating of all was the ritual Jewish oath (*more judaico*), instituted during the reign of Prince Mihai Sturdza in 1838 and which continued in use until 1919. This oath, taken in a synagogue, consisted of a bath of purification, reading from the Torah, blowing of the ram's horn, and texts in Hebrew or Yiddish guaranteeing the truth of the testimony to be given. Sometimes this oath was extracted by the authorities in a cruel manner, as in one case, that of a certain Joseph Goldenthal in 1868, who had to take the bath of purification in freezing water, fast for 24 hours and have his nails cut down to the quick.

It must also be mentioned that in nearly all of the anti-Jewish riots, they began or ended in pillage of the synagogues and violation of the scrolls of the Law. Distrust of the Jews "who had killed God" and practiced "ritual murder" was reinforced by a clever denunciation of the Jewish religion itself.

The former revolutionary of 1848 César Bolliac transformed his newspaper *Trompeta Carpatilor* into a well-known anti-Jewish platform. On December 30, 1869, he told the Chamber of Deputies that:

> This congregation is so far from wanting to assimilate with the people among whom they live as a real parasite that they imagine they have a separate God and they pray this God be harsh on foreign nations. Some people say that in Romania the Jewish question is a religious question. Others deny it. We must understand each other. When one speaks of Catholics, Protestants or Orthodox, we are speaking of Christian people who have received their teaching from the same source: the Gospel. When one speaks of the Jews it is of people who do not believe in Christ and who, consequently, do not have the same religion as we have. So it is impossible to talk about the Jews without implying their religion, because when you ask them why they do this or that they always answer that their religion requires it. Thus in this sense one cannot say that the Jewish question is not a religious one.

Although this opinion of a "democratic" politician and the facts cited above show that religious tension was one of the causes of the rise of anti-Semitism, it is nevertheless true that this phenomenon grew from the top down because of other factors.

2. The Economic Factor

We have already pointed out that the Jews contributed effectively to the growth of cities in Moldavia, to the expansion of trade and the creation of the first industries, acting as a middle class. Their role was described by a Moldavian Deputy, Costache Epureanu, himself a large landowner, in a brilliant speech before the Chamber when Article 7 of the Constitution was being debated. He said:

> Since 1832 when the Danube waterway was opened and the soil began to be exploited, it became necessary for us to have a middle class between the growers on the land and outside consumers, a commercial class to collect the products and export them. In Wallachia there are no Jews, but there were Bulgars, Greeks, Armenians; in Moldavia, which is closer to Russia and Galicia, the Jews arrived. This is how one can explain that our economic development brought foreign elements into our society.
>
> If these foreign elements are here because of the historical development of our political economy, if we have been forced, so to say, to admit them, now that they are today established, have bought houses, why should one want to stop their trade and why should they not have today the rights which they have had and which they enjoy under present legislation and which, besides, will return them to the situation where they were a hundred years ago? ... From the economic point of view, the Jew, as the sole possessor of capital, is useful to society and not only causes no harm to it, but is even useful.

But the position of the Jews in the country's economy was being denounced by Dionisie Pop Martian, who called for complete nationalism and a protectionist policy, i.e., discriminatory.

In 1866, another writer, Bogdan Hasdeu, a former professor of statistics in the lycée at Jassy, published as essay entitled *National, Foreign, and Jewish Industry and the Principle of Competition*. He expressed some of the ideas of Martian which opposed economic liberalism. He concluded that free exchange between nations was "a slavery for the weak." He said that even open competition between the nationals of the same country would be paralyzed if the country contained foreign industrialists or those of "a different character." He denounced the Jews as causing economic trouble within the state because of three negative qualities: "the tendency to earn without work, the lack of a sense of dignity, and hatred against all nations."

The real source of this opposition lay in the changes which Romanian society had undergone, in the creation and growth of a national bourgeoisie. It was economic competition and a spirit of narrow-minded exclusiveness which transformed the young Christian bourgeoisie into the most persistent enemy of the Jews and of their emancipation. The position of the Jews as "middle classes," in business and in the trades, was henceforth in danger. One deputy, I.C. Codrescu, accused the Jews brutally during a speech before the Chamber of being the "sharks of the middle class." Addressing himself to the Jewish community, he said: "If you realize that our struggle is not against your religion, but against your desire to monopolize the middle class of our society, tell that to Europe, to the foreign governments to which you are sending your complaints."

Speaking before the Chamber of Deputies on June 29, 1875, Petre Carp, Minister of Public Education, considered the Jewish question in a different way. He said: "Do you want to obtain victory in your struggle with the Jews? Work hard, be thrifty like them and you will have nothing to fear. What I said then I repeat today. The solution to the Jewish question lies in competition at the workplace."

As they were looked upon as dangerous and undesirable, it is not surprising that most of the administrative measures, laws and circulars aimed at shutting the Jews out of the areas of activity to which they were confined. Let us remember that the Thirty-One Project wanted to deny them any means of existence. The Jews were systematically rejected or eliminated from all the economic corporations which were created at that time such as *La Prévoyance* (insurance), the Economic Fund, the Pension Fund, Mutual Insurance. The extent and effectiveness of this struggle against the Jews in the economic sphere grew out of the new electoral law of the Constitution of 1866 which changed the Jewish question into a parliamentary and political one.

3. The Political Factor

Far from being equitable, the electoral law left power in the hands of the boyars by dividing the electorate for the Chamber of Deputies into four colleges and by ruling out the largest part of the population, namely the peasants. But at the same time it introduced representatives of the new bourgeoisie onto the political scene, giving them a sizable quota (20). The total number of deputies from the third college composed of businessmen, industrialists and the free professions was 58. The three other colleges (composed as follows: the first college of those having an income of more than 300 ducats from real estate; the second college of those with an income of at least 10 ducats; the fourth college included citizens not included in the other categories) only totaled 99 deputies.

Using a power which they had not had before, the members of the third college set about inflicting a series of exclusions on the Jews. The Senate, which was a conservative body composed of 69 senators, always followed the Chamber of Deputies in voting the anti-Jewish laws. During the electoral campaigns, measures against the Jews doubled in intensity in order to win the favor the voters.

At an electoral campaign meeting held at Jassy on August 26, 1876, the rector of the university in that city, Nicolae Ionescu, who was also the Minister of Foreign Affairs, declared:

> ...We have amongst us a non-Christian people, the Jews, against whom we are struggling in vain. To rid ourselves of this national plague, we must send to the Chamber free men who are not dependent on any Jewish purse and they will have to make a solution of the Jewish question possibly by deciding, in the name of the Romanian nation, that the government should issue free passports and even some financial aid to the impoverished Jews living in Romania, so that they may leave for their country, Palestine, leaving the Romanians sole masters of the trade which the Jews have dominated.

This statement was eloquent in explaining the role of anti-Jewish propaganda among the citizenry and also the outlook of the candidates for election to the Chamber. Delaporte, the French Consul at Jassy, explained in a despatch at the time of the "Thirty-One Project" why the persecution of the Jews was the work of the government itself: "The Ministry is using it as means to gain popularity with the masses, or rather with the voters in the city colleges who are all people fanatically against the Jews."

The first five years of the Hohenzollern regime were characterized by great instability in the government: there were ten changes in the government and thirty cabinet reshuffles. In the first elections in 1866, Conservatives obtained a majority in the Senate and Liberals in the Chamber. The government of Ion Ghica, set up after the elections, consisted of Conservatives and moderate Liberals. After his resignation on March 7, 1867, there were a mixture of Conservative and Liberal governments. Finally, the Conservatives remained in power from 1871 until 1876.

The Liberal governments were supported particularly by the Liberal and Independent Fraction which was composed of the small and middle Moldavian bourgeoisie. Its leader was Nicolae Ionescu, referred to above. His ideology reflected that of Simon Barnutiu, a professor at the College of Law in Jassy. He supported exclusive nationalism, democratic-middle class republicanism and redistribution of the land among the peasants.

The action of the Fraction which led to disturbances against the Jews was criticized by the conservative journal of Jassy, the *Gazeta de Jasi*, and even the journal of the radical liberals, *Perseverenta*, attacked the chauvinism of the Fraction. But most of the press (of 126 newspapers, 110 were political) was hostile to the Jews, painting them in the darkest colors. Whereas the expulsion circulars of 1867 and 1869 were the work of members of the two sections of the Liberal Party, the law on the sale of spirits and other similar measures, on the other hand, were brought by Conservatives. Thus, with respect to the Jews, the two "historic" parties, in spite of some difference in form, held one and the same attitude.

Prince Carol von Hohenzollern, without being especially favorable to the Jews through his background or his education, showed himself well disposed towards them from the beginning of his reign. Touched by the extent of the repercussions the disturbances had evoked in Europe, Prince Carol denied that they had a religious aspect and in his official statement was lavish in his reassurances. In reality, he stood behind the anti-Jewish policies of his ministers and regretted their departure, like that of Bratianu in 1867. During a trip to Moldavia in 1867, he told L. Castaing, the French chancellor at Jassy, that he was astonished by "the large number of Jews in the country and was shocked by their physical look." He said that he had "found them in the mountains, far from any town, and their exterior which was usually dirty, was repulsive to me as I saw that the peasants in the mountains seemed to be well off and clean." This effect of the traditional Jewish costume on the Romanian prince brings us to a final subject which must be taken into account: xenophobic nationalism.

4. The Xenophobic Factor

The difference between the countries of western Europe and eastern Europe in the development of modern nationalism was brought out by Yaacov Talmon in his book *Destin d'Israël*. Whereas in the West, the organization of the state was generally imposed from above and by force and united its divergent elements before the rise of nationalism, the same did not happen in the East. The Israeli professor pointed out that where, for centuries, the Welsh have not tried to separate from England, and the separatist tendencies of the people of Provence and of Brittany were limited to demonstrations of "regional narcissism," Russia, Austria, and Turkey did not succeed in bringing the different ethnic groups together before the rise of nationalist aspirations. The persistent struggle of the oppressed nationalities of the three empires stems from this. Nationalism is also a "state of mind" and a kind of "conscience," an ambivalent idea. A result of this ambivalence is that nationalism is both a "conservative force" and a "revolutionary factor." "Nations established as states," he wrote, "are generally inclined towards conservative nationalism, while those struggling against foreign dynasties or colonial powers to gain their independence naturally turn towards revolutionary nationalism."

This postulate, insofar as our study is concerned, finds its best illustration and confirmation in the history of Romania. For a long time, the Romanian people lived under the yoke of three empires: Turkey, Austria, and Russia. The awakening of Romanian nationalism which took place in a striking way during the revolution of 1848 was based on the ideas of union and independence. For the Romanian patriots of 1848, nationalism was a revolutionary factor and in their struggle for independence and union, the Jews were considered as "Jewish brothers" who could contribute effectively to the accomplishment of their dreams.

The creation of a Romanian national state through the union of Moldavia and Wallachia (without Transylvania, Bukovina and Bessarabia, which were attached to it after World War I) changed the nationalism of the veterans of 1848 into a "conservative force." It is with this in mind that we must interpret the xenophobic attitudes of the Romanian nationalists. They were also the result of the antagonism which existed between the backward socio-economic conditions of the country and the ideology of romantic liberalism imported from France.

The Romanian peasant, guardian of the language and the ancestral traditions and customs, represented, in the eyes of the revolutionaries of 1848, the very conscience of the Romanian nationality and many writings called for improvement of his condition. But the promises contained in many revolutionary tracts were not fulfilled in the autonomous state, for, despite the agrarian reform of 1864, the situation of the peasants grew worse through exploitation and plundering which increased to the point where their only *raison d'être* was to pay taxes and supply soldiers to the army.

The former revolutionaries of 1848, having become the political framework of the new regime, called upon the West, where they themselves had mostly been trained, to modernize the country. Thus modernization became a synonym for "Westernization."

A large number of craftsman, skilled workers and engineers appeared on the staffs of various foreign economic missions which assumed responsibility for building railways, factories, prospecting for petroleum, and setting up port facilities. With the feverish investments of western capitalists, certain clear-thinking individuals understood at that time that the country was in danger of losing its economic independence. The equation "modernization = Westernization = colonization" was confirmed later on.

Moreover, the Romanian nationalists were alarmed when they became aware that in all of the new companies the managers were always foreigners and the unskilled workers were always Romanians, former peasants who had left one miserable life for another. This fact was also noted by certain foreign observers and in 1876 Eugen Weber, as Austrian expert, expressed his doubt as to the capability of the Romanians to create industries themselves. The Romanian nationalists asserted, on the other hand, that a normal economic development could take place if the country got rid of the foreigners.

The Jews were also looked upon as foreigners, although many and lived in the principalities for generations. Because of their language, dress, religion and customs which set them apart, especially in Moldavia, from the rest of the population, they were the most hated group. The politicians of the period constantly accused them of being a danger to Romanian nationality because of their large number and non-assimilation.

In 1866, during the parliamentary debate on Article 7 of the constitution, Ion Bratianu had said that "It is not so much the characteristics of their race as their large number, which means that our nationality is threatened and if, as a consequence, it has to take measures to defend itself, it is not intolerant but farsighted."

Mihail Kogalniceanu had justified his expulsion circulars as an effective way to defend Romanian nationality.

For the deputy I.C. Codrescu, the term "Romanian Jew" had no meaning and was an insult to the Romanian people. "The term 'Romanian Jew' is nonsense, because the Jew belongs to one nationality and the Romanian to another, and just as one cannot speak of a Romanian Frenchman, Romanian Englishman, Romanian Turk, one cannot speak of a Romanian Jew. Either one is Romanian or one is a Jew. No one can belong to two nationalities."

There is no doubt that the xenophobic factor fueled hatred against the Romanian Jews and continued to turn them into simple foreigners, a burden and a scourge for the young national country.

To conclude, anti-Semitism prior to 1878 was religious, socioeconomic, political and xenophobic. There was not yet an organized ideological movement, but the official policy of persecution finally turned the Jews into stateless people. Little by little, the principle was accepted that there were no Romanian Jews. To have a complete picture of relations between Jews and Christians before 1878, we must make a quick critical survey of the changes that took place within the Jewish communities.

CHAPTER FIVE

PORTRAIT OF THE
JEWISH COMMUNITY

An overall sketch of the daily life of the Jews in the middle of
the nineteenth century and up to the First World War lies outside the
limits of the present study. However, let us try to describe its essential characteristics prior to the Congress of Berlin in a short résumé.

1. Ashkenazi and Sephardic Jews: Clothing, Language, Names, Habitat, Occupations

In the middle to the last century the Jews of the Romanian
principalities were not a homogenous community and one must first
of all distinguish the Jews of Moldavia from those of Wallachia, and
among the latter, between the *Ashkenazim* and the *Sephardim*.

At that time all the Jews of Moldavia, with a few rare exceptions, were Ashkenazis, that is, Jews who by their origin, whether
natives or of distant or recent immigration, were related to their co-
religionists in Poland, Russia, Germany and Austria-Hungary by
their language, their names, their religious prayers and customs.

The Moldavian Jews have always been greater in number than
those of Wallachia, representing a majority of about 90% in 1859
and about 75% in 1899.

Half of the population of Jassy, the Moldavian capital, was
Jewish in the 1850s and one observer wrote that it could be called a
Jewish city, because, he said, "one sees the Polish costume a lot in the
streets and intersections of this strange city which is hardly seen any
more in the large cities of Poland and Russia."

This brings us naturally to a description of the Jewish costume.

Clothing

In the first half of the last century, the Moldavian Jews wore a
costume which was unique, showing the influence of the Turks and
the surrounding milieu both by its different parts and by its colors.

The men's workday dress consisted of a sleeveless coat
decorated with frogs and worn over a white shirt. The trousers were
wide and held by a large belt which one finds among the Galician
Jews. The head was covered by a bonnet made of light material,
lined in cotton and sewn in squares. The base of the bonnet was

covered by a strip of white material which could be removed for washing.

Holiday dress was finer. The men wore a long caftan which came to the ankles and had green and blue stripes (green was the usual color of the Turkish costume). The caftan was closed around the neck by a frogged collar and buttons; the cuffs had the same decoration. The wide belt, like that of the peasants, held the hand-kerchief, spectacles or tobacco pouch and, if need be, ink in a tin box and a holder for goose quills.

Over the caftan, they wore the *fermenea* - a coat of heavy stuff reaching down to the waist; it was lined in the winter and covered by another coat, the *giubea*, reaching to the ankles and sometimes lined with sable. Finally, over the *giubea*, there was long, wide cape in black rep silk, like that worn by monks.

The head was covered by a cylindrical headdress of felt with a shawl turban of Turkish influence or a sable bonnet covered with velvet.

From the middle of the nineteenth century, the Moldavian costume was replaced by the "Polish" under the influence of Jews coming from Galicia, who were more orthodox, but only for holidays.

The Polish dress was a black caftan, held at the waist by a black belt of embroidered silk. The classic *shtramel* was worn on the head, a bonnet with thirteen angles of sable fur.

The women's dress was not different from that of the non-Jewesses. On the head they wore a fez with silk fringes tied together by a linen turban. In time the fez was replaced by a strip of satin covering the head, reflecting Serbian influence.

On their wedding day, according to tradition, the girls cut off their hair and covered their head with a fichu and later with a wig.

It is interesting to note from a contemporary who found a cause for resentment in the men's costume that: "The peasant is too narrow-minded and mistook the Jew in his special dress for the same Jew who had crucified his Savior 1,800 years before, because he saw in popular pictures a similar figure, similarly dressed, representing the Lord. This was the effect of that special costume."

The Polish costume was gradually abandoned both by the choice of the Jews themselves, especially the younger ones, and by the wish of the authorities.

In two successive circulars, in April, 1859, and in May, 1860, Mihail Kogalniceanu, then Minister of the Interior, asked the Moldavian rabbis to use their authority to convince their congregations to replace their traditional dress with the "European" one. Translated into Hebrew and Yiddish, the circulars were distributed by the thousands throughout the Jewish communities. This greatly weakened the resistance of the extremely orthodox *hassidim* and a considerable number of young people began to wear modern clothes. In the next decade, the Polish costume disappeared except among a small number of Orthodox Jews.

In contrast to Moldavia, the costume of the Ashkenazi Jews of Wallachia had been largely "Europeanized" by the middle of the nineteenth century; only older people occasionally wore the Polish dress. The Sephardic Jews of Wallachia, descendants of those who had formerly been expelled from Spain, have always been few in number, both in comparison with the Ashkenazi Jews of Romania and the Sephardic Jews of the neighboring Balkan states. As we have seen above, their origin lay in the sixteenth century, but a few families immigrated in the eighteenth and beginning of the nineteenth centuries from Turkey, Bulgaria, and Serbia.

At first, the costume of the Sephardic Jews was that of the Turks, but it changed in time to be more like the national dress of Wallachia. Only the rabbis, called *haham*, retained the Turkish costume. Young people adopted French clothes which at that time were considered the latest style in Wallachia. After marriage, a young woman who dressed in the European manner kept her clothes, but covered her hair with a small red bonnet, the *fez*, surrounded by rows of little gold coins, as in the Orient.

Language

In the middle of the nineteenth century, although Romanian was widely used by the Jews, their usual language in Moldavia was Yiddish and in Wallachia it was either Yiddish or Judeo-Spanish.

The Ashkenazi Jews of Moldavia spoke Yiddish, a Judeo-German dialect with many borrowed words from Slavic and Romanian sources. In that language, which is considered by many to be a bad jargon, there grew a press, a literature and drama which were extremely rich. We shall speak of that later. It still continues in our time to be the second language of the Romanian Jews.

On the other hand, Judeo-Spanish was less successful in its growth and a recent book on the phonetics of Judeo-Spanish published in Paris by Marius Sala in 1971 states that in that year only 150 persons in Romania could speak it. Only one regular periodical appeared in that language between 1885 and 1887, *El Luzero de la Paciensia*, edited at Turnu Severin by a certain Rabbi Crespin as an organ for the early Zionist movement Ichoub Eretz Israel. It used Latin characters. Another appeared in the same town in 1894 with the Hebrew title *Har Sinai*.

Patronymic Names

Besides the Hebrew origin which forms their base, the patronymic names of the Romanian Jews came from three different sources. It was not until the nineteenth century that these names became official in public records (the *état-civil*) as a result of socio-economic changes (the development of trade, taxation, military requirements).

The first source concerns Jews of ancient origin who lived together of a long time with the native population and borrowed from the Romanian language either the ending of their Hebrew names or even Romanian names with specific endings whose meaning indicated their occupation or their geographic residence, as for example:

- escu: Avramescu, Isacescu, Iocabescu
- eanu: Aroneanu, Ocneanu, Podoleanu, Focsaneanu (from the town of Focsani)
- aru: Ciubotaru (bootmaker), Fainaru (miller), Sticlaru (glazier).

The second source relates to the Ashkenazi Jews of Moldavia whose ancestors came from Poland, Austria-Hungary or Russia and who had received specific names when civil records (the *état-civil*) were introduced into their respective countries by the Prussian law of 1812, the Austro-Hungarian Imperial laws of 1785 or the Imperial Tsarist statute of 1804.

Under the Austrian law of 1785, the Jews had to change their names into German patronymics or those of German structure. In the eastern parts of the Empire local authorities, for mercantile reasons, distributed the names by categories according to the meaning of the compound words, selling them for sums of money. This explains how certain persons received names which included special terms, such as:

- Ehre, Krone, Schön, Süss
- names of precious metals, such as Gold, Silber
- names of flowers, like Blumen, Rose
- some strange names such as Pfeffer, Beutel, Pulver, Schwanz

Or names of trades or geographical localities:
- Kaufmann, Drucker, Hafner, Binder, Tischler, often with the suffix "er."
- Berliner, Frankfurter, Wiener, Kissinger.

The third source characterizes the Sephardic Jews. Among them we find names which are
- Spanish: Alcaly, Behar
- Italian: Mitrani, Graniani
- Arabic: Aftalion, Alfanderi
- Greek: Papo, Semo
- Turkish: Medina, Nahmias.

Habitat

Different from other countries and especially the Occident, the Romanian Jews never lived in real ghettos. However, in the large cities they lived in several sections - in Jassy in Targul Cucului, Podul Ros and in Bucharest in Dudesti and Vacaresti.

The houses in which they lived were not very different from those of the Christians of the same level. Sometimes there were noticeable differences between the homes of rich bankers and the un-hygienic houses or even hovels of the small tradesmen and craftsmen. Through subscriptions and the generosity of social leaders the Jewish communities built synagogues, schools and hospitals which were architecturally outstanding.

Occupations

A detailed and chronological study of the social structure and the role of the Jewish population in the economic development of Romania has still to be made. Let it suffice to say that by the middle of the nineteenth century they constituted the majority of craftsmen and merchants in Moldavia. Before being prevented by various laws, many Jews owned cabarets and lent money at interest especially in the small towns and villages where there were no banks.

During the 1860s, some Jews held important places in high-level businesses and in banking and they were among the first to create large industries. Besides these and some physicians and engineers, prior to 1878, most of the Jews were involved, as we have pointed out, in trade and handicrafts. At the end of the nineteenth century and the beginning of the twentieth, as a result of economic changes in the country, there was a change in the Jewish population through the emergence of a proletariat.

2. Demographic Evolution

First of all, we must note the demographic progress of the Jewish population in Romania during the second half of the nineteenth century which, though not reaching 500,000, as stated in anti-Semitic periodicals, was nevertheless quite large. The only reliable census reports were made in 1859 for Moldavia and in 1899 for all Romania, which then included Moldavia, Wallachia and Dobrudja.

According to the census of 1859, the total population of Moldavia was 1,325,096 of which 118,922 were Jews. To this number must be added 5,945 Jews in the districts of southern Bessarabia who were returned to Romania after the Paris Congress in 1856. The geographic distribution shows us that most of the Christian population lived in the country side, while the majority of the Jews were living in the cities, particularly the district capitals, some of the towns and a small number of villages.

The population of Wallachia, according to a statistical report of 1860, was 2,400,921, of which 9,234 were Jews (5,934 in Bucharest; 3,108 in the other cities; and 96 in the countryside).

According to these figures, in 1859-1860, the Jews represented 9% of the Moldavian population, 0.4% of the Wallachian and about 3% of the two principalities together.

In 1800, the population of the Kingdom of Romania was 5,912,520, of which 269,115 were Jews. In Moldavia, of a population of 1,832,106, there were 195,887 Jews. In Wallachia, of a population of 3,822,172 there were 68,852 Jews.

In 1899 Jews represented 10.5% of the population of Moldavia, about 1.8% of the population of Wallachia and 4.5% of the overall population of Romania. Comparing the statistics of 1859 and 1899, we can draw the following conclusions:

(1) The Jewish population in the Moldavian countryside remained almost identical after 40 years (16,019 against 12,279); in rural Wallachia, the number of Jews was negligible (958 against 96). This stagnation stemmed from the official policy of keeping the Jews away from the land. Although they were sometimes tolerated, they were often expelled in a harsh way.

(2) In Moldavia, the increase in the number of Jews over 40 years was 76,750. In Wallachia, the increase was 59,618. The demographic movement in Wallachia was due to internal migration from Moldavia towards the capital.

(3) The Jewish population has always lived in the cities and to a lesser extent in small towns. So the geographic distribution of the Jews confirms a law of modern Jewish demography which refers to the Jews as the "most highly urbanized people in the world." The increase in the number of Jews in the cities was especially felt in the last two decades of the nineteenth century.

There was no census taken in 1878, but the total number of Jews is estimated at about 200,000.

After 1899 and until World War I, there was a decrease due to emigration and the natural movement of the Jewish population. According to the census taken in 1912, Romania had a total population of 7,900,000 of which 239,967 were Jews, or about 3.3%, divided geographically as follows: 167,590 in Moldavia, 68,253 in Wallachia, and 4,124 in Dobrudja. The Sephardic Jews were not counted separately; in 1919 their number was estimated at about 10,000.

Because of the lack of detailed statistics showing the evolution of the different classes of the population over a span of 40 years, a quantitative study of the social history of Romania in general and of the Jews in particular in very difficult. The progress of the Jewish population in Romania in the last half of the last century was different from that of the Christians. The flux of the Jewish population followed the ascending curve of Jewish demography in Europe. As in other countries, in Romania the great demographic revolution of the nineteenth century was more startlingly apparent among the Jews.

3. Disorganization of Community Life

The increase in the number of Jews was not accompanied by a strengthening of the Jewish communities. On the contrary, an actual disintegration of community structures may be noted. Following the government decision of July 3, 1862, to no longer supervise the internal organization of the Israelite communities, Jewish community life began to be affected.

Because of the income from the tax on kosher meat, which was often considerable, the institutions created and supported by the communities, such as schools, hospitals, asylums, and places of worship, were able to operate almost normally for still a few years after that decision, but after another decision in 1866, the Jewish communities lost their civic character. The government authorities took no part in the election of the community leaders and refused to help the administrators collect the tax on kosher meat. Since the latter was no longer as mandatory as before, the revenue constantly decreased, affecting the maintenance of community institutions. On May 5, 1869, the president of the Israelite community of Bucharest, Adolphe Waimberg, wrote to the Romanian Minister of the Interior, Mihail Kogalniceanu, deploring this situation and requesting that the community again be placed under the aegis of the government.

A similar request was made by the leaders of the Jewish community of Jassy, but these petitions received no reply and Romanian Judaism lacked a community organization capable of defending its interests for the rest of the century.

The new government policy strengthened the opposition between the Orthodox and Modernist parties which often appeared to be a schism. In some communities management came into the hands of the Orthodox *hassidim*, who refused to subsidize the Israeli-Romanian schools created and encouraged by the Modernists, as they preferred to teach the Hebrew religion in the traditional *hadarim*. In the Israeli-Romanian schools, which were short-lived after 1866 because they depended on the generosity of philanthropists, Yiddish was the language of instruction, except for the schools of the small community of Sephardic Jews in Wallachia, but besides the Hebrew language, the language and history of Romania were also studied there, thus hastening assimilation. These schools were necessary at the beginning because parents refused to send their children to the state public schools which were gradually opened after 1866 due to the hazing of which they were the target and also due to the opposition of Orthodox Jews. However, the number of pupils in the state-operated schools - there were only about 30 before 1866 - continued to grow and reached about 7,500 in 1882. Still, that was a small number in view of the whole Jewish population of school age.

In order to maintain some cohesion within the communities, several intellectuals and leaders in Bucharest founded in 1872 the *Infratirea Zion* (Zion Fraternity) which received constant support from Benjamin Peixotto. That organization aimed at uniting all of the Jewish communities of Romania to improve their organization and open schools. It grew rapidly and four years after its establishment had twenty branches in the larger communities. In 1875, following a petition, that fraternity whose motto was "Fraternity, Charity, Education" was authorized by the Council of Ministers as a philanthropic society. In a relatively short time it succeeded in founding and subsidizing schools, hospitals and other charitable institutions. The departure of the American Consul in 1876 and the war of 1877-1878 dealt it a serious blow; it lost resources and was forced to cut off aid to nearly all of its activities. Although this association represented a first attempt, partially successful, at preventing the dissolution of community institutions, it could not alone replace a structured society and fill its needs without resources other than philanthropic ones.

Despite its impoverishment and disorganization due both to government policy and internal division, the community (*ha-kehila*) remained all through the nineteenth century the base and foundation of Jewish life. After 1878 the struggle to attain recognized community organization expanded, but the authorities constantly opposed it, alleging that the community was the greatest obstacle to assimilation of the Jews.

4. Isolation and Integration

Facing the political and social ostracism which they suffered, the Jews did not cease their efforts to leave their isolation, to modernize their way of living and become part of the country.

But the socio-economic structure of most of the Jewish population was such that their integration into Romanian society could only be that of a minority. In fact, except for a small number of leaders (bankers and wealthy merchants) who were assimilated

and a small middle class of merchants who were more or less assimilated, most Jews lived from manual work in great isolation. They
were tailors, cobblers, tinsmiths, cabinet makers, upholsterers, lathe
turners, roofers, coach builders, blacksmiths, stevedores, cesspool
cleaners, etc. - a class of craftsmen and proletariat with the
characteristics of an underdeveloped population. Between 1866 and
1878 we can observe a process of urban concentration due in part to
expulsions from the rural areas which increased competition and the
impoverishment of large sections of the Jewish population. This was
also due to the fact that the Jewish craftsmen, who had been much
sought after until the 1860s, were replaced through the superiority
of German, Austrian and French workers who had come to live in
Romania. Because of their socio-economic position, the cultural
world of the Jews was not unified and, except for a small class of
intellectuals and famous rabbis, the Jewish masses presented a
mixture of religious traditions and ignorance. However, the atmo-
sphere of the *shtetl*, the small village with a large Jewish population,
began to be disturbed in the 1860s by rationalist ideas coming from
Bukovina and Bessarabia, the two frontier provinces of the Austrian
and Russian Empires where there were large Jewish communities.

The Russian trend towards *haskalah*, which encouraged a
revival of the Hebrew language and a national Jewish culture, and the
Austrian trend towards assimilation met and fought against each
other in Romania. It is remarkable to note that the Yiddish theater
was able to rise from the sands of an intellectual desert and the
relatively spiritual stagnation of a Jewish life which was at risk.

The first professional Yiddish theater in the world opened in
1876 at Jassy, directed by Avram Goldfaden, the father of the
modern Jewish theater. The Yiddish theater was a cultural institution
of a secular nature. It was feared by the Orthodox Jews and
criticized by the assimilated ones who thought it represented an
obstacle to emancipation. The historian Moses Schwartzfeld took this
significant position: he was glad for the creation of this type of
drama, but he wanted it to be played in Romanian, "the language of
the country," instead of Yiddish. Despite this and other criticisms,
this theater grew and had a fine career. It sprang from the spiritual
need of a population who lived in a special cultural environment.

The beginnings of Jewish journalism up to 1878 also give
evidence of the isolation of the Jewish people, of their difficulties,
but also their progress in assimilating the Romanian language.

The first Romanian newspapers were published at the time of the Organic Law in 1829, one in Bucharest and another in Jassy. The first Jewish newspaper appeared twenty-six years later at Jassy. Written in Yiddish, *Kort Haitim* (Events of the Time) attempted to popularize the idea of emancipation among the Moldavian Jews. Two years later came the first Jewish newspaper in Romanian, *Israelitul Roman*, with columns in French written by Armand Levy, fighting for political emancipation. This weekly periodical only lasted for six months, but it was the first of a series of bilingual Jewish publications, which generally did not last very long. They were in Yiddish and Romanian, in Romanian and French, and in Romanian and Hebrew. Then, in 1872, there appeared the first paper solely in Romanian, *Vocea Aparatorului* (The Voice of the Sentinel).

The Jewish press in Romanian experienced its real blossoming after 1878 through a new generation of intellectuals trained in Romanian schools and through progressive assimilation of the Romanian language by wide sections of the Jewish population. This press dealt with all the ideological trends in Judaism, from extreme Romanization to nationalist isolationism.

In spite of their isolation, the Jews showed their attachment to Romania during the War for Independence. During the campaign of 1877-1878 there were 883 Jewish soldiers out of a total of 35,000 in the Romanian Army. The Jews fought brilliantly and many Jewish soldiers were decorated and their names appeared after the war in lists published by the *Moniteur officiel.*

The contribution of the Jews to the War for Independence was not limited to the battlefield. Across the country, a series of committees were formed to collect gifts of money and in kind (clothing, underwear, horses, cattle). The *Call to the Jewish Women of the Capital* asked the women to "give the maximum to help the soldiers who have been wounded in this great battle for the future of our country."

There was no delay in answering these appeals and Romanian newspapers were quickly filled with lists of subscriptions by Jews from all parts of the country. The Zion Fraternity contributed four ambulances and placed them under the patronage of the reigning princess. The Jewish community of Jassy opened two hospitals, one in Bucharest and the other near the field of battle at Turnu-Magurele. Many welfare associations, with the Jewish communities, contributed a great deal to the war effort. The heads of the Jewish banks of Michel Daniel et fils in Jassy and Hillel Manoach of Bucharest were decorated with the Star of Romania for their exceptional work.

When the war was over, the Romanian Jews rightfully hoped for a change in their situation, a cessation in persecutions and the granting of political rights. Such a change would be announced by the Congress of Berlin where it was proposed by the French delegates.

CHAPTER SIX

THE CONGRESS OF BERLIN AND NON-EMANCIPATION

1. Romania and the Jews in the Wings of the Berlin Congress

The Russo-Turkish War of 1877 was a sequel to the failure of the Conference of Constantinople in 1876 to regulate the situation in the Balkans. That war, declared by Russia on April 24, 1877, had as its stated aim the emancipation of Christians in the Ottoman Empire. It was said that "we are not marching for conquest but to defend our insulted and oppressed brothers, to defend the Christian faith."

This was said by Grand Duke Nicolas to his army before crossing the Prut River towards the battlefields of Bulgaria. We do not intend to judge the motives which pressed Russia to begin hostilities. Let us only note that besides the old idea of a crusade against the infidel, the Tsarist Empire also had interests in that area.

Romania, still a vassal state, seized the opportunity to attain its independence. On April 4, 1877, Mihail Kogalniceanu, Minister of Foreign Affairs, signed with Baron Demetri Stuart, Russian councilor and Consul General at Bucharest, an agreement which allowed the Russian army to cross Romanian territory.

The independence of the country was proclaimed on May 10, 1877, the anniversary of the accession of Prince Carol. He took command of the army himself and crossed the Danube to help the Russian army, which suffered many defeats after a few victories. One by one, the Turkish forts fell before the victorious advance of the Romanian Army. On November 29 Osman Pasha turned the city of Plevna over to Prince Carol and on February 12, 1878, the Romanian Army entered Vidin in northwest Bulgaria, on the Romanian frontier.

But Romania was not even invited to attend the peace talks as her reward. The Romanian government learned of the Peace Treaty of San Stefano on March 3, 1878, from the newspapers of Moscow. Articles 5 and 19 of that treaty related to Romania. In the first, Turkey recognized Romanian independence; in the second, Romania was to cede southern Bessarabia to Russia and receive in exchange part of Dobrudja. Thus, by seizing a beautiful and rich region, the Tsarist Empire compensated its ally for its decisive share in its victory over Turkey. Discontent over this arose at once in Romania. Nor were the Great Powers satisfied with an arrangement which was taken without their consultation. The idea of a European congress to create the basis for a durable peace in the Balkans quickly arose. As early as February 5, 1878, Austria sent a circular note to the Powers which had signed the Treaty of Paris in 1856 and the London Protocol of 1871 proposing an international conference so that Europe might agree on the changes which had become necessary to make in those treaties. Russia refused at first but finally accepted because of the unanimous agreement of the other Powers.

The Berlin Congress began on June 13, 1878, with the participation of Germany, Austria-Hungary, England, France, Italy, Russia and Turkey.

Romania expected two things from the Congress: recognition of its independence by the Great Powers which had protected it since 1856 and prevention of the seizure of southern Bessarabia. The Romanian Minister of Foreign Affairs, Mihail Kogalniceanu, and the Prime Minister, Ion Bratianu, went abroad as representatives. Prior to the start of the Congress, Bismarck intimated to Bratianu that the cession of Bessarabia was essential. The Jewish question was also raised and Bratianu replied that he was preparing a draft law aiming at the emancipation of native Jews and that foreign Jews might obtain naturalization on an individual basis. But this was only a way to avoid the problem. In July, 1877, Kogalniceanu had promised emancipation of the Jews to representatives of the Jewish Alliance of Vienna. From February, 1878, the end of the Turkish War, and up to the beginning of the Congress in June, 1878, the Romanian government did nothing in that direction.

Well aware of the domestic situation in Romania and the position of the government and the legislature there, powerful Jewish organizations such as the Universal Jewish Alliance, the Anglo-Jewish Association, the Israelitische Allianz of Vienna, the Romanian Committee of Berlin, the Board of Delegates of American Israelites, and a number of well-known Jewish leaders started at the end of the war a broad campaign aimed at the freedom of the Jews. This campaign also extended to Serbia and Bulgaria and involved the press, the parliaments and governments, urging that the Berlin Congress make a forceful decision of this matter. Baron Gerson von Bleichröder, a banker and personal advisor of Bismarck, played an important role in this, writing to the Central Committee of the

Jewish Alliance in Paris and indicating that he was in contact with both Prince Bismarck and Baron Alphonse de Rothschild, who would encourage France, Austria and Russia to agree with Germany that it was in the interest of Europe to require equality before the law for all religious groups in the former Turkish provinces.

The petition from the Jewish community of Berlin and from other communities was well received by Bismarck. On February 28, 1878, an official reply was sent in his name to the Jewish community of Berlin, containing this promise: "...when the negotiations now in course at the Congress concerning the peace treaty present the opportunity, the German delegate will be asked to support all efforts made to grant to the members of all religious groups in the countries concerned the same rights as those guaranteed to them by the German constitution."

Adolphe Crémieux turned to M. de Saint-Vallier, the French ambassador to Germany, who answered obligingly and said:

> ...Mr. President, I hasten to reply to your letter with its enclosures and to assure you that if the Congress meets and if I am called to participate in it, I shall consider it a duty to justice and human-ity to carefully seek ways to improve the status of Jews in the East according to the old and generous traditions of French policy. Besides, I know that I shall be guided in this direction by my honorable chief and friend, M. Waddington, the Minister of Foreign Affairs....

As the beginning of the Congress drew near, there were many initiatives in favor of the Balkan Jews. The questions were brought up in the parliaments of Germany, Italy, France and England. In Austria-Hungary, Count Gyula Adrássy assured Jewish leaders that at the Congress his government would defend the principle of equal rights. On May 23 Baron von Bleichröder wrote to the Central Committee of the Alliance that "the time has come to prepare for the future Congress by having the major newspapers carry articles in favor of tolerance." On the same day he wrote to Crémieux that "in its own interest Romania will be obliged to accept emancipation of the Jews which will certainly be proposed by the Congress."

There came an important result from these difficult negotiations when, on June 5, 1878, the minister of the United States in
Austria, Mr. John A. Kasson, suggested in a note to Secretary of
State Evarts that the American government intervene vigorously to
have the Congress proclaim equality of rights for the Romanian
Jews. In particular, he asked that recognition of Romanian independence should depend on the granting of civil rights to all inhabitants
without distinction. He wrote: "That all subjects or citizens under the
jurisdiction of the Romanian government shall, irrespective of their
race or religion, have equal rights...."

On June 13, 1878, Sir Moses Montefiore sent a memorandum
to the English representatives at the Congress; the Central Committee
of the Alliance sent one to all the delegates to the Congress and also
sent three representatives to Berlin - Charles Netter, Saki Kann, and
Veneziani - to make contact with members of the Congress. Rejected
by the delegates from Serbia and Romania, they were well received
by those of the Great Powers.

Encouraged by the assurances they had received in the wings
of the Congress, these various organizations awaited the outcome.

2. Article 44 of the Berlin Treaty

During the debates at the Congress, the French representative,
William Henry Waddington, the Minister of Foreign Affairs, was the
first to raise the question of equal civic rights for all the inhabitants
of a country, independent of their religious affiliation. This was
during the fifth session during a discussion of the Bulgarian question
and the Congress accepted the article proposed by the French
delegate which imposed religious freedom on Bulgaria. In the
meeting on June 28, after the independence of Serbia had been
agreed upon, Lord Salisbury asked that religious equality be
stipulated. Waddington supported that and proposed that the independence of Serbia be recognized on the condition that, like
Bulgaria, it proclaimed complete liberty of worship and equal rights
for all inhabitants. All delegates accepted the French proposal except
Prince Gortshakov, who said: "...If we are speaking of civic and
political rights, we must not confuse the Jews of Berlin, Paris,
London or Vienna, who certainly should not be refused any political
right, with the Jews of Serbia, Romania and a few Russian provinces
who are, in my opinion, a real scourge for the local population."

Finally, despite the insistence of the Prince, the independence of Serbia was agreed upon under the condition of religious freedom. From June 29 on, the Congress dealt with the Romanian question. Prince Gortshakov opposed admitting the Romanian delegates, but had to give in to the will of the majority. During the session of July 1, Ion Bratianu and Mihail Kogalniceanu outlined Romania's historic rights to Bessarabia and asked that the independence of their country be recognized. Unfortunately, the seizure of Bessarabia was considered a *fait accompli*. Waddington declared that the French delegates were asking the Congress for Romanian independence, but under the same conditions as those of Serbia relative to the principle of equality of rights. His proposal was accepted by the Powers and the work of the Congress concerning Romania is contained in Articles 43, 44 and 45.

Article 43: The High Contracting Parties recognize the independence of Romania subject to the conditions expressed in the two following articles:

Article 44: In Romania, the difference in religious belief cannot be held against anyone as a reason for his exclusion from, or unfitness for, the exercise of civic and political rights, admission to public office, functions and honors, or the operation of different industries and exercise of different professions in any region whatsoever.

Freedom and the public forms of all religions are guaranteed to all nationals of the Romanian State as well as to foreigners and no obstacle shall be placed in the way of the hierarchical organization of the different faiths or in their relations with their spiritual leaders.

The nationals of all Powers, businessmen or others, shall be treated in Romania without distinction of religion on a footing of perfect equality.

Article 45 stipulated the return to Russia of southern Bessarabia in exchange for Dobrudja with its frontiers rectified by Waddington.

The text of Article 44 left no room for doubt: it called explicitly for equal civic and political rights for the Jews. Thus, by this article in the Berlin Treaty, there was an honorable solution to the Jewish problem in Romania. Cardinal Franchi, Papal Secretary of State, sent a letter of appreciation and compliments to Waddington, a Protestant, for his work and the principles of religious freedom contained in the Berlin Treaty. Crémieux sent warm telegrams of thanks to Waddington and Saint-Vallier. Echoing the feeling of all French Jewry, S. Bloch, editor-in-chief of the *Univers Israélite*, wrote on August 1, 1878: "So it is again mainly due to France and its delegate to the Congress that the holy cause of freedom of conscience will triumph in regions which are still half-civilized. We are happy and proud as Jews and as Frenchmen."

How was Article 44 received in Romania? What was the attitude of the government, the legislature and the press? What was the reaction of the Jews and how was their emancipation effected?

3. Emancipation or Naturalization?

Attitude of the Government and the Legislative Bodies

The attitude of the government and that of the legislative bodies was easy to imagine and cause no surprise. Having fought against the insertion of Article 44 in the Treaty, it was clear that the government would not at once accept its stipulations. On the contrary, it tried by all means possible to avoid granting rights to the Jews. It tried to obtain international recognition without literal compliance with Article 44 through intense diplomatic activity including circulars, letters, memoranda and even sending ministers abroad.

At first the government headed by Ion Bratianu attempted to obtain such recognition even before the Chambers had been officially informed of the text of that article and before any decision was taken concerning it. Mihail Kogalniceanu, the Minister of Foreign Affairs, wrote to Waddington, his counterpart in France, asking for the accreditation of a Minister Extraordinary and Plenipotentiary prior to the start of the legislative session, but France, like the other signatories of the Berlin Treaty, refused to undertake anything before being certain that Romania would change its policy towards the Jews.

On November 27, 1878, the Chambers began work on "the new events." On the same day, Prince Carol, in his address from the throne, spoke for the first time during his reign of the Jewish question:

> The country has been called upon to convoke Chambers of Review which alone have the right to change the articles of the constitution. They must answer through constitutional channels the expectations of Europe and satisfy the moral question which the Romanians themselves have to erase from the constitution: the principle of political inequality because of religion, which is no longer in harmony with the philosophy of the century.

Thus the Prince was asking for a change in Article 7 of the constitution which contained the well-known discrimination on religious grounds, but without explicitly stating his thought and without mentioning whether a real change would take place in the situation of the native Jews. But his thinking was expressed in a letter to his father in which he said: "The Jewish question can only be arranged by a constituent assembly. I intend to call such an assembly during the winter in order to remove from the constitution the article relating to this. It is clear that this delicate question cannot be clarified except by giving the Jews in the future the ability to ask for political rights as for any other foreigner."

So all the Jews were looked upon as foreigners. This idea even guided the government and the Chambers which found an excellent pretext for not resolving Jewish emancipation. Since the Jews were all foreigners, in order to enjoy all rights, including political ones, they had to be naturalized as Romanians. Thus it was only necessary to change Article 7, which prohibited the naturalization of non-Christians, to show the good will of the government to conform with Article 44 of the Berlin Treaty. Since naturalization could only be obtained on an individual basis through a special law, the subterfuge and bad faith of the authorities can easily be understood. However, this argument was successful and increased the laxity of the government.

On November 29, 1878, C.A. Rossetti left the government and was sent to England, France and Italy to ascertain the intentions of those powers with respect to Romania. A few days later Ion Bratianu resigned and the Prince asked him to form a new cabinet with a more homogeneous outlook. Ion Campineanu became Minister of Foreign Affairs instead of Mihail Kogalniceanu, who was no longer in the government.

The correspondence between Varnav-Liteanu, the Romanian diplomatic representative of Romania in Berlin, and his Minister of Foreign Affairs is one of the most important for understanding the position of the Romanian government and that of the Great Powers.

As early as September 29, 1878, he warned against any postponement of the emancipation of the Jews. He wrote: "It is my duty to tell you that hesitations and delays will be of no avail. By withholding the great principle of equality of rights and by prolonging that exception in our laws we are certain to lose all respect in Europe."

On January 8, 1879, following an interview with von Bülow, he wrote that Romania's recognition by the Powers would only take place after the legislative chambers had acted for revision of the constitution and reform of the institutions in conformance with the Berlin Treaty.

In an important letter of January 18, 1879, the Romanian diplomat mentioned the tendency of his government to assimilate all Jews with aliens and to delay the granting of equal rights *sine die*:

> Several newspapers have asserted cleverly that all Jews in Romania are foreigners, with the result that it would seem sufficient to give them political rights, those of asking the legislature for naturalization. I do not hesitate to say that this way of arranging the question would be looked upon by the Great Powers as demurrage.... The words 'nationals of the Romanian state' used in Article 44, as opposed to the word 'foreigners' is clear proof that the Berlin Congress did not want Jews who are nationals of Romania to be considered as foreigners.

In closing, he cited the French Revolution as an example: "Far from causing trouble, this reform would be an advantage.... By admitting them to the bosom of the great nation...they will blend with us and be good Romanians just as they became good Frenchmen when the great revolution proclaimed their emancipation...."
However, with a few exceptions, the debates held in the legislature were quite different from the Liberal views of Varnav-Liteanu. It should be pointed out that the two Chambers postponed until March 12, 1879, their decision as to the need for revision of Article 7 of the constitution and therefore the need for a constituent assembly which the government had requested in January. During that interval and until May 6 when the Chambers were dissolved to make way for the future constituent bodies, very passionate debates took place concerning the Jewish question. They indicate the determination to avoid solving the problem according to Article 44. The following speech by the deputy Nicolae Fleva was one of the most important and well received:

> And as far as I am concerned, I have the courage to say from this podium that I shall never consent to all of the Jews having political rights. (Applause.) And I do not think there is a country which would ask for that if injustice went so far as that Europe should ask for such a thing; in that case the Great Powers would first have to step over my body before obtaining my support for the death of my fatherland.

The various speakers stressed that one must point out to the country how the Chambers of Review should solve the problem, namely only by special and individual laws. M. Voinov stated this position before the Senate on May 10, 1879, as follows:

> To avoid any risk, we must motivate our resolution and show the Chambers of Review that by rescinding Article 7 we want to protect Romanian nationality.... It must not be thought abroad that we shall naturalize the Jews *en masse* or even by categories, when it is clear that they can only be

naturalized on an individual basis, choosing the
best among them.

Elections for the constituent assembly took place amid lively
agitation and resulted in the victory of the Liberals, whereas the
Conservative opposition only received eight members in the Senate
and seven in the Chamber of Deputies.

The Chambers of Review were opened on June 3, 1879, by a
message from the Prince which was devoted almost entirely to the
Jewish question. For the first time, Prince Carol supported the
theory of the Jewish invasion and spoke of the danger which that
"foreign element" represented for national economic development.
According to him, that was the reason for legislative restrictions
such as Article 7 concerning the Jews. He said that those restrictions
had not succeeded in their purpose and, on the other hand, had exposed the country to unjustified accusations of religious intolerance.
For that reason, he was now proposing a change in the constitution
which would not contravene "the most vital interests of the people."

His address showed the direction which the debates were to
take: the non-solution of emancipation. By embracing the principle
that no one could be deprived of any right because of his religion, he
said that "We shall satisfy the main dictates of Article 44 of the
Berlin Treaty. But in matters of detail, the Great Powers are not and
cannot impose absolute solutions on us contrary to our most vital
interests."

The new Chamber appointed a commission to draw up a draft
law to replace Article 7 of the constitution. The text presented by
that commission specified that naturalization could only be granted
on an individual basis by a law voted by the Chambers and with a
probationary period of ten years.

Germany, England, France and Italy expressed their displeasure and asked Austria to urge the Romanian government to insert
Article 44 of the Treaty into the constitution in place of Article 7. It
refused and reacted to the note from the Austro-Hungarian cabinet
by a text accepted by the Prince. Differing from that of the
Chamber, which only stipulated individual naturalization, this draft
provided emancipation to several categories of Jews: those who had
done their military service as required by law or who had served on
active duty; those who had obtained academic degrees in Romania or
had attended the first five classes in a modern or classical lycée;

those who had provided the country with works on education or of a philanthropic nature; those who had published a book in the Romanian language; those who had established factories except distilleries. The Bratianu government resigned on July 16 and was followed a week later by a coalition ministry which included two Conservative ministers, B. Boerescu for Foreign Affairs and N. Kretulescu for Public Works, Trade and Agriculture.

Boerescu summarized the policy of the new cabinet in a circular letter sent on July 25 to Romanian legations and diplomatic agents abroad. He said: "We declare formally that the principle of Article 44 has been accepted by the Romanian nation. It only remains to put it into the execution which cannot be done, the Great Powers will understand, except within the limits of what is possible." According to him those limits were of those of individual naturalization, for the emancipation of all Jews "would be a terrible blow to all the economic interests of the country.... It would certainly push the residents to despair, revolt and God knows what other misfortunes."

On August 3, 1879, Boerescu was charged by the Prince to contact the major capitals of Europe to obtain recognition of his country's independence. Like the earlier mission of C.A. Rossetti, this one was unsuccessful.

The French press covered Boerescu's mission amply, but its tone was reserved, skeptical and generally in opposition.

After the summer vacation, the parliamentary session began on September 16, 1879, and three draft laws were presented to the Chamber of Deputies. One proposed naturalization by categories, the second individual naturalization and the third was completely opposed to a change in the constitution. These three drafts, all of which were finally rejected, gave rise to lively debates on the Jewish question. The new parliamentary session was a replay of the preceding one and the most implacable enemies of Jewish emancipation freely vented their resentment and there was a pseudo-scientific discussion, the sole purpose of which was to prevent changing Article 7. As before, the only one to express a Liberal opinion on the Jewish question was Petre Carp, but his speeches brought little reaction from the hostile assembly.

On September 24, Minister Boerescu presented the government's own draft law. It contained acceptance of the principle of Article 44, namely that differences in religious belief or membership constituted no obstacle to the acquisition and exercise of civic and political rights. Native Jews appeared therein as "Romanian subjects." This draft only provided for *individual naturalization*. Its only novelty was a list of those who would be immediately naturalized.

The government project was denounced and the extremists even refused to accept the phrase "Romanian subjects" which was given to native Jews. The famous list of "assimilated" Jews who could be naturalized at once only contained the names of 1,075 candidates, including the 883 soldiers who had taken part in the Russo-Turkish War. It was more than laughable and even then many deputies opposed it and it was not debated.

To better understand the outcome of the question and the vote on the new Article 7, we must recall briefly the position of the Jews themselves.

Attitude of the Jews

After the Berlin Congress, the leaders of the Jewish communities and various welfare associations adopted a wait-and-see attitude and waited for the application of the principle contained in Article 44. In view of the turn taken by the debates in the Romanian parliament, the native Jews sent a petition to the Chambers of Review filled with many expressions of beautiful patriotic sentiment. It was not taken into consideration at all and there was no discussion of it. For the Jews, the only hope for emancipation lay in the intransigence of the Great Powers. After the presentation of the draft law on September 24, the Romanian government exercised pressure to obtain individual requests for naturalization in order to prove to the Powers that the native Jews accepted the principle of individual naturalization. Only a small number requested naturalization, as the Action Committee, made up of Jewish leaders, opposed the individual requests. At the same time parliamentary deputies hostile to the government plan contacted the Action Committee and suggested the immediate naturalization of 3,000 persons in addition to those who had fought in the War of Independence. A deputy named Heraclidi, a well-known opponent, made that proposal on the condition that the Jews sign petitions, like those of other *foreigners*, as the most important point for him and those he represented was not to recognize the Jews as native nationals. The representatives of the Action Committee protested, but finally accepted the principle of this compromise. That was a serious mistake and contributed to a large degree to the non-resolution of the problem. During the negotiations, agitation grew among the Jews and the Jewish newspaper *Fraternitatea*, in a bitter article entitled "Representatives without Mandate," accused the members of the Action Committee of having betrayed the cause of the Romanian Jews.

Nevertheless, certain members of the bourgeoisie who were well off and assimilated took an opposite view, hoping to be future Romanian citizens.

The idea of naturalizing 3,000 persons at once did not come up because the committee refused to *buy* the 12 votes required for passage of that project which would have amounted to about 300,000 francs.

After more bargaining, a new draft law was finally voted and became the new Article 7. This article, which did not provide for emancipation of the Jews, and whose exact significance will be dealt with later on, and whose exact significance will be dealt with later on, ended a period of real government crisis during which politics were constantly agitated by a virulent anti-Jewish campaign carried on largely by the press.

Attitude of the Press

During that period which extended from the end of the Berlin Congress in July, 1878, to the promulgation of the new Article 7 in October, 1879, the Romanian press did not cease handling the question of emancipation of the Jews.

Both the government-oriented papers and those of the opposition objected from the beginning to the right of the Great Powers to interfere in a matter which they looked upon as purely Romanian. This only resulted in an increase in national feeling and more hostility toward the Jews. Most newspapers published many articles placing the Jews in a most unfavorable light, as though they were responsible for all the ills from which the country suffered, the attacks in the press, and the calumnies of which they were victim. The insults became especially violent as people began to realize that a solution to the problem of emancipation had to be found. The only way indicated in most of the papers was the need to change Article 7, but in a "national" direction which made emancipation practically impossible.

The government newspaper *Romanul*, managed by C.A. Rossetti, wrote at the close of the Berlin Congress:

> The Jewish question was handled and solved like that of Bessarabia: the Jews were placed on the same level as the Russians, as controllers of the will of the Romanian nation. If the powers of Europe thought that by doing that they were rendering a service to the Jews of Romania, they will be bitterly deceived; on the contrary, nothing could so harm the cause as the Congress resolution....

In August and September, 1878, before the opening of Parliament, the unofficial Liberal paper *Telegraful*, ran several articles on "The Berlin Congress and the Jews of Romania." Here were some of its views:

> The Congress decided to place the Jews of Romania on the same footing of equality and rights as all the civilized countries of Europe! This was doubtless done through ignorance of the situation, because they do not know the Jews, either what they are, nor their number in the country, where every vagabond and former prisoner has come to live and whose number is more than half a million out of a population of scarcely four million. This proportion does not exist in any other country. If the members of the Congress had ever traveled through beautiful Romania and had seen the Jewry of this country, we are certain that not only would they not have insulted us by placing the Jews on the same level with us, but they would have advised the Romanians to rid themselves of this disease which does not exist anywhere as it does here. Romania has begun today to be no longer a Romanian land but rather a Palestine like that of a few thousand years ago.... At Passover time they seize a Romanian

child which they stab in order to withdraw its blood....

On September 26, 1878, *Romanul* wrote of the need to revise the constitution, but substituted for emancipation the principle of individual naturalization. After having convoked a constituent assembly and after having debated the issue, there would have to be "detailed inquiries to determine the number and political situation of the Jews...foreign Jews have to be separated from Romanian subjects and among the latter, one has to determine how many were born in this country...and who would consequently be qualified for naturalization under the same conditions as foreigners and how many would want to be emancipated in that way as foreigners do who wish to be naturalized...."

L'Orient, a French-language newspaper, made many absurd and slanderous accusations against the Jews. A paper in Marseilles, *Le Sémaphore*, published a refutation on March 12, 1879, saying in part:

> ...If the Romanian Israelites are reduced to the miserable state which arouses the scorn of *L'Orient*, is that not the fault of those who despise them and exclude them with brutal violence from the political community? In France, England, Germany, in all self-respecting countries, the Jews who receive so little consideration in Bucharest have reached the highest positions through intelligence and work.... Since the Jews pay the taxes in Romania which other citizens pay...they must not be refused the rights recognized by the constitution for residents of the country....

The satiric weekly *Perdaful*, in Jassy, full of anti-Jewish caricatures, published on April 15, 1879, a notice threatening the Jews, who were presented as cosmopolitans and as a disease aiming at the destruction of the beautiful Latin race. The author wrote that the Jews must not insist on obtaining rights, because, he said, there are limits to the patience of the Romanian and he will struggle even against the will of Europe.

When the Chambers of Review opened in June, 1879, the attacks against the Jews in the press became more urgent.

On June 11, 1879, *Romania libera*, the organ of the Minister of the Interior Mihail Kogalniceanu, wrote:

> Who can force us to take to our bosom a half million charlatans to suck our blood, become owners of our property and then treat us as slaves in our own country? That will never happen. The Romanians will not give in no matter what pressure is brought to bear upon them by foreign powers supporting the Universal Israelite Alliance. The Jews are a sword with its point in the ribs of Romania, while the hilt is held by the Israelite Alliance.

On June 12, *Pressa*, a Conservative newspaper wrote:

> Finally let us imagine the impossible, that the signatory powers of the Berlin Treaty, without taking our rights into account or any of our arguments, became angry with us and decided to destroy us. Then, it is better to die as Romania than as Palestine. It is better to die under the Krupp cannons than infected by the Jewish disease. Better to die as a free country than as a slave nation.

Timpul, an organ of the extreme right of the Conservative Party, ended its article of July 3rd on the Jewish question as follows: "The only thing we can grant the Jews and which we shall help to give them without difficulty, is a hemp noose and gallows in sufficient quantity for them."

On July 29, *Telegraful* expressed threats against the Great Powers and the Jews, saying: "Can the Great Powers compel us to commit suicide? Can they use force to impose on us a solution which is not agreeable to us? Let them do it. But we assure them that when foreign armies cross our borders, the Romanian people will have themselves buried all the Jews." ("Buried" is a pun which also means "to make them native.")

Renascerea, a Liberal newspaper, described the role of the new cabinet in its supplement dated July 22:

> The role of the new cabinet has been set in advance: it must use all its wisdom, all its experience, all its influence to make clear to the legislative bodies and Europe the true face of the Jewish question. It must show some that Romania cannot commit suicide because it pleased certain poorly informed diplomats to insert an inexplicable clause into the Berlin Treaty which is incorrect in spirit and above all humiliating.... It must show others that no country won by leaving open questions that foreigners can use to interfere in the nation's business....

Ecoul Terrei published an open letter to the Prince asking him to prevent the Jewish Alliance from turning Romania into a "black Palestine."

From October, 1879 on, *Romania libera*, Mihail Kogalniceanu's paper, published the by-laws of the anti-Semitic League which had been established in Germany and regularly reproduced, like other newspapers, articles and excerpts from German anti-Semitic publications.

This short overview of the Romanian press is suggestive: after one year anti-Semitism had become part of the Liberal and Conservative press.

4. The New Article 7 of the Constitution and Recognition of Romanian Independence

The new Article 7 of the constitution was adopted by the Chamber of Deputies on October 19 by a vote of 122 to 9 and by the Senate on October 23 by a vote of 56 to 2. It was promulgated by the *Moniteur Officiel* of October 25, 1879:

> Article 7: Distinction of religious belief or membership will not constitute in Romania an obstacle to the acquisition of civic and political rights and their exercise.

Paragraph 1: A foreigner, whatever his religion and whether he stands under foreign protection or not, can be naturalized under the following conditions:

a) He sends his request to the government, stating his capital, the profession or industry in which he works, and his desire to establish a domicile in Romania.

b) Following such a request, he must reside in the country for ten years and prove by his actions that he is useful to the country.

Paragraph 2: The following may be excused from this period of probation:

a) Those who have brought industries or useful inventions into the country or who have outstanding talents; those who have established large business or industrial enterprises.

b) Those who, having been born and raised in the country, were never under foreign protection.

c) Those who served in the armed forces during the War of Independence; these may be naturalized collectively at the request of the government, by a single law and without other formality.

Paragraph 3: Naturalization can only be granted by a law on an individual basis.

Paragraph 4: A special law will determine the manner in which foreigners may take up domicile in Romania.

Paragraph 5: Only native or naturalized Romanians may acquire rural property in Romania. Rights already acquired will be respected. International agreements which already exist remain in force with all their clauses until the expiration date.

This new text, while beginning by stating the principle of Article 44 of the Berlin Treaty, only deals with individual naturalization. From that time on, even foreigners of non-Christian faith, could acquire Romanian citizenship under certain conditions and by a special and individual law. Instead of being granted by the Prince as before, it would henceforth be given by a vote in the parliament. What was the situation created for the Jews? Although their name was not mentioned therein, this article set their new status. Although up until then they had been considered Romanian subjects (a term used in Boerescu's project) - an incorrect, insufficient and exaggerated expression to define the citizenship of the native Jews - they became henceforth "foreigners not standing under foreign protection." This hybrid formula transformed all the Jews in Romania into stateless persons. It contributed in a decisive way to keeping the Jewish problem acute.

However the solution reached by the Romanian cabinet displeased the Great Powers. Waddington protested and the Romanian representative in Paris, Callimachi-Catargi, wrote to his minister: "In conversations I have had with various persons, they were generally dissatisfied with the outcome. They feel that the difficulties have been deferred rather than solved. To correct that impression, it would be good for the number of naturalizations, which should be voted on at once, to be rather large."

Since another revision of the constitution was not probable, the Romanian government was asked to make an official statement to guarantee execution of Article 44 of the Berlin Treaty. The Bucharest cabinet agreed and sent the following statement to the Great Powers:

> Article 7 of the constitution of Romania, incorporating the principle of Article 44 of the Berlin Treaty, has given the Jews access to citizenship and abrogates all existing laws contrary to that principle. Its observation will continue to be sincere and honest. The organic authorities will take care to insure its respect and apply it in order to reach, as a consequence, a more and more complete assimilation of the Jews, and to discontinue the restrictive system which has been set up with respect to foreigners concerning rural property. Meanwhile, all Jews residing in the country will have, from the standpoint of private civil law, an assured juridical status, without having to fear arbitrary administrative measures

or special laws because of their religion. As a
matter of course, all foreigners of determined
nationality will receive fully equal treatment
without any distinction because of their particular
religion.

At the same time, the parliament, by a single law, granted
citizenship to the 883 Jewish soldiers who had taken part in the war
against Turkey. Then Italy recognized the independence of Romania.
France, England and Germany did not follow that example.
Waddington declared in the Chamber of Deputies on December 15,
1879, that he did not think the time had yet come to recognize its
independence.

Whereas France and England were guided in their policies
towards the Romanian government solely by humanitarian consid-
erations and their support of the principles expressed in the Berlin
Treaty, that was not the case in Germany. From the correspondence
of Varnav-Liteanu, the Romanian diplomatic agent in Berlin, it
appears that the Jewish question had become in the hands of the
German government a means for pressure to solve the famous affair
of the Romanian railways. The loan needed for building a railway
system (about 914 kilometers) was only placed in Germany, where
stockholders were recruited among the wealthy Prussian aristocrats,
but also among small investors. The shares of stock suffered constant
devaluation. To preserve the interests of the German investors (about
100,000 marks), Prince Bismarck insisted that the Romanian
government buy back the devalued securities at a very high price. On
November 21, 1879, Boerescu reported to Prince Carol that he had
received a despatch from Varnav-Liteanu according to which the
German government had decided that the Romanian government
could not be considered as having solved the Jewish question unless
the agreement on the railways was accepted as quickly as possible.
To obtain the support of Germany, the Romanian government agreed
to buy back railway stock at a price nine times higher than that at
which it was listed. That agreement was voted by the legislature on
January 27 and Germany became the most reliable supporter of
Romania.

Bismarck hastened to inform the French and English governments of his intention to recognize Romania and asked them to let
him know their positions. After some hesitation, France and England

finally gave their consent. The three chanceries agreed to proceed simultaneously to recognize Romanian independence by means of a collective note drawn up by the French government.

On February 20, 1880, the representatives of Germany, England and France sent to the Romanian government a note which recognized the independence of the Principality of Romania without condition, expressing their readiness to establish regular diplomatic relations with that country.

As that recognition had been accepted immediately after the Berlin Congress by Turkey, Austria, and Russia, by this note Romania joined the concert of independent nations.

A new era began for independent Romania which became a kingdom in 1881. It was also a new era for the Jews, as their juridical status was changed by the new Article 7. Not only was the principle of emancipation, which was supposed to solve the Jewish problem in Romania, not accepted, but in addition, it became through this article a weapon in the struggle against the Jews. By defining the Jews as *peregrini sine civitate*, it contained the germs for a policy of legislative discrimination which was systematically directed against them. The task of the legislator was facilitated by this for, from then on, he could legislate not against the Jews, but against foreigners who were not "protected by a foreign power." For the Jews this was the real outcome of the Berlin Congress.

The former minister, C.A. Rossetti, one of the most outstanding men of the new kingdom, declared in *Romanul* on December 25, 1881: "The Romanians can congratulate themselves for having solved the most burning and dangerous question in a national way - and now we can admit that it was contrary to the manifest will of the Great Powers and even contrary to the spirit of the Berlin Treaty."

CHAPTER SEVEN

ANTI-SEMITIC LEGISLATION

1. A System of "Government Rotation"

In order to better understand the Jewish problem after the Berlin Congress, let us examine briefly the socio-economic and political changes in the country.

There was an appreciable upswing in agriculture, which was the base of the Romanian economy. Agricultural production increased 100% between 1866 and 1906. In 1912, cereal grains and byproducts from them represented 75.7% of exports and just before the First World War, agriculture, which involved 85% of the population, supplied more than 2/3 of the Gross National Product. Despite this growth, which was reflected also in the prices of agricultural products, the living standard of the Romanian peasant remained very low; far from improving, his situation grew constantly worse. This was due to the fact that agriculture was dominated by large landowners and the quasi-feudal relations between them and the peasants. Statistics from the end of the century show that more than a million peasants owned less land than a few thousand large landowners. Whereas 4,171 large properties had an area of 3,787,192 hectares, 1,015,302 peasants only owned 3,319,695 (about 3 hectares per person).

Although several laws were passed in 1878, 1881 and 1889 allowing the purchase of state-owned land by the peasants, the lack of land forced them to continue to farm that of the large landowners or of the intermediate landowners. The latter became a real class of entrepreneurs and large-scale producers who expanded their management over larger and larger areas. At the beginning of the twentieth century, they controlled 62% of the properties of more than 100 hectares in Moldavia. Quite a few Jews acquired an exceptional position in this field, such as the Fischer brothers of Jassy who monopolized the cultivation of 138,424 hectares in 1904. This was exploited by the nationalists to channel the anger of the peasants who suffered from what one scholar called neo-slavery. Their exploitation and poverty pressed the peasants to rebel, as they did in 1888 and, on a larger scale, in the great revolt of 1907.

The agrarian problem and the Jewish problem were the two important social problems which the Romanian governments did not know how, or did not want to solve before the First World War.

Industry advanced through the creation of plants and factories in the capital and the Danubian ports. At the end of the nineteenth century the number of large and medium manufacturing plants was listed as 279 and just before the war, the assembly plants counted 847 firms. But the development was uneven - a rise in the extraction sector (oil), slow growth in metallurgy - and industry occupied a secondary place both in the Gross National Product and particularly in exports.

Transportation and communications developed regularly and at the beginning of the twentieth century railroads reached 3,500 kilometers and motor roads 27,000. This helped increase the volume of domestic and foreign trade, the latter being greater in the period 1901-1915. Trade also increased during the same period. The National Bank was founded in 1880, with the right to issue paper money. This was followed by other banking institutions of various categories. Foreign capital, particularly German, counted for the largest investments.

The bourgeoisie grew stronger at the expense of the Jewish merchants and craftsmen because of its exclusivity. There also appeared a proletariat which became conscious of its own interests and tried, after 1893, to find an organization and political expression. But these socio-economic changes did little to affect political life. The country continued to be governed by an oligarchy of large landowners, joined by some wealthy bourgeois.

After the recognition of its independence, the Principality of Romania became a Kingdom. Prince Carol assumed the title of Royal Highness on May 22, 1881, and all the Great Powers recognized the new kingdom. It was a paradox that the Liberal government, whose members had worked in 1848 to establish a republic, proposed this change. It was probably to refute accusations of republican tendencies after the assassination of Tsar Alexander II on March 13, 1881, that Ion Bratianu made that decision.

The electoral law was changed in 1884, but changed the body of voters very little. It created three colleges to elect deputies to the parliament. The first consisted of large landowners and high finance; the second, attorneys, judges, professors, etc., and the third, everybody else. The inequality was obvious. In the first college of 77 deputies, there were 15,000 who voted; for the second college of 72 deputies, 33,000 voted; and for the third college of 40 deputies, there were 1,029,000 voters of whom 53,000 voted directly and 976,000 voted indirectly. The last, representing the majority of the people, only elected a quarter of the members of parliament.

It was in this climate that the rotating Liberal and Conservative governments vied with each other in the number and seriousness of laws enacted against the Jews.

2. Naturalization Policy

Under this system of "government rotation" the emancipation of the Jews, solemnly promised to the governments of the Great Powers, remained a dead letter.

From 1879 to 1900, only 85 persons were naturalized, 27 of whom died during the same period.

In 1913, besides the veterans of 1877, the total number of naturalizations after the Berlin Congress was 529. This increase was due to the Jews of Dobrudja. In fact, the government decided in 1909 to grant political rights to the residents of that area who had formerly been Turkish subjects. After some hesitation, the authorities also included the Jews, but because of administrative difficulties in proving their former Turkish nationality, only some profited from that decision.

The applications always caused passionate debates in the parliament on the Jewish question. One of the first and most famous occurred in 1880 concerning Daniel, a native Jew who founded the oldest bank in Moldavia. The naturalization of Adolphe Stern, one of the leaders of the Romanian Jews, also met with strong opposition in parliament and it was only through his literary works that he was just able to obtain the necessary majority in the Chamber of Deputies.

Among those who were naturalized, some had to pay large sums of money to the senators and deputies in order to enter the "Romanian nation." The system of individual naturalization, which gave the members of parliament absolute power, encouraged corruption. In early 1911, a group of twelve deputies was created which proposed naturalizing 3,000 Jews in exchange for large sums of money. Their agents went through the Jewish communities to "register applications" and, of course, to extort money.

We do not know the number of requests for naturalization submitted between 1879 and 1919, but it certainly amounted to several tens of thousands. Those requests often remained in the dust of the archives for twenty and even thirty years awaiting their turn.

The case of Professor Lazar Saineanu, originally Schein, who revolutionized Romanian philology through his widely recognized studies, and who was refused naturalization after twelve years of struggle and hope, is typical of the way in which the government envisaged solving emancipation. This is how he sketched his personal drama after having had to leave his country for France:

> It is an extremely painful page in the history of contemporary Romania which I am offering here for the reader's meditation. He will find here impartially told the sad and humiliating vicissitudes through which one must pass who aspires to become a Romanian citizen, the only right which can protect a man from arbitrary expulsion from his own country. The case is typical. Here is a man who was born in the country, was raised in the schools of the country, was honored by the best institutions of high culture, who was Professor in the University and the Normal School, who is the author of scientific work which brings honor to the Romanian name; you think that this is more than sufficient to obtain the rights of a native citizen? Don't you believe it! For 12 years he will be the victim of arbitrary regulations which have taken the place of law, the target of perfidious attacks by a band of blind chauvinists. Here is a résumé of the illegalities committed against him: having been twice rejected and once admitted by the Senate, he was first received and then rejected by the Chamber; these admissions and rejections were voted on under legal conditions which were absolutely identical. And that criminal game with the basic law of the country, that express violation of the constitution by the very persons who are called upon to observe it, lasted twelve long years; a sad comedy, playing with the life and future of a man and ending with the final exclusion of a *Romanian* philologist from

Romanian nationality. And that is how a man of
science, after having devoted all the enthusiasm of
his youth and all the strength of his maturity to
Romanian language and literature, finds himself
compelled after 40 years to wander in search of a
fatherland....

The non-solution of emancipation and the cynical policy on
naturalization was only one of the aspects of the anti-Jewish stance of
those in power. In the period from 1878 to 1916, physical attacks
were no longer as frequent as before, but on the other hand, legal
oppression was increased by means of legislation.

It is not our intention, and it is not our task, to report all the
laws and circulars which were voted at that time against the Jews,
amounting to more than 200. Nevertheless, we think it necessary to
present the most important ones in the three following fields:
military, education and economy.

3. Military Laws

It was military service which bothered the authorities the most
and prevented them from assimilating the Jews to "foreigners."

Several laws governed the enrollment of Jews in the Romanian
army. Under the law of June 11, 1868, they were called to the colors
as "Romanians," but from 1876 on, they were called up as
"foreigners not of foreign nationality."

The Berlin Congress and Article 44 of its final treaty brought
a change in attitude. The government, fearing justifiable claims,
decided to take away from the Jews the trump-card of military
service, intending to avoid at all costs the granting of equal rights.
Many secret circulars called for complete exclusion of Jews from the
army. Young Jews were refused military service and in addition they
were required to sign a statement of renunciation which ran as
follows:

I, the undersigned, born at ..., and residing in the
city of ..., at ... Street, state that I am the son of a
non-naturalized foreigner and consequently I
request exemption from the military service in

Romania, as I never want to place myself under Romanian protection.

After recognition by the Great Powers, there was a new change in the government view. From 1882 on, Jews had to serve in the army not as "Romanians" or as "foreigners not under the protection of a foreign power," but as "residents of the country." The principal articles of the law on army recruitment dealing with the Jews were the following:

> Article 1 - Personal military service is required of all persons who reside in the country.
> Article 2 - Subjects of foreign countries cannot serve in the army. The sons of foreigners, born in the country, cannot be exempted from military service if they have not accomplished it in another country.
> Article 63 - All Romanians may voluntarily enlist in the army.
> Article 66, par. 4 - In time of war, all young men of 18 may voluntarily enlist for the duration of the campaign.

In the army, Jews could not attain the grade of officer, and from 1895 on, in many regiments they were refused even the grade of corporal and non-commissioned officer.

Jewish physicians and pharmacists had to serve in the army as private soldiers (Romanians served one year with the rank of lieutenant).

The regulation on internships in military medicine, dated August 15, 1898, provided in Article 6 that only military medical students might have internships - that is, Romanian students, naturalized Romanians, or those born to parents naturalized *before their birth.*

The decision relative to conditions for admission to the Institute of Military Medicine for the year 1908-1909 provided:

> Article 1, par. 2 - For admission to the competition, candidates must send to the Institute of Military Medicine a request with the following

enclosures: ... c) a certificate from the city hall of their place of residence affirming that they are the sons of Romanians or naturalized Romanians. In the latter case, they must also enclose the *Moniteur Officiel* in which the law pertaining to their father's naturalization was published.

Jewish members of the military services cannot be appointed as clerks of military courts (Article 3 of a regulation dated February 18, 1990).

Jews could neither enter the rural gendarmerie nor the military schools.

The decree concerning the conditions for appointment to a public post under the Minister of War, dated August 12, 1914, stipulated:

Article 1 - No one can be appointed to a public function under the Ministry of War if, besides the other conditions required by that Ministry, he is not a Romanian citizen.

All of these disqualifications (the list is not complete) show that even within the army Jews were subjected to a system of exception. The newspaper *Jüdische Presse* published in its May 26, 1887, edition the following words of General Manu, a member of the Romanian Senate, relative to the situation of Jews involved in military service: "When I was a student in the school of cadets in Berlin, I was considered Prussian, and after graduation, I again became Romanian; similarly, the Jews are Romanians, that is, subject to military service, and after leaving the army they again become foreigners."

We may conclude by stating that military legislation proceeded from a desire to classify the Jews as foreigners, without having to take regard of the military service itself. On the other hand, legislation on the schools tended to degrade the Jew, making it more difficult for him to take part in modern life, preventing his assimilation. This result was to be obtained by gradual eviction from the schools.

4. School Laws

By Article 23 of the Constitution of 1866, education in the state schools was declared free and without cost.

Although at fist, as we have seen, parents were reticent and only occasionally sent their children, one result of the tolerance of the authorities was a genuine rush of Jewish children to those establishments.

In 1878-1879, Jews represented 11% of the total number of pupils in the public elementary schools in the cities and 30 to 50% in certain localities. Four years later, these rose to 15% and in certain cities from 30 to 75%. In five years, the number of Jewish pupils in the different state schools almost doubled.

The increase in the number of Jewish pupils and their thirst for knowledge disturbed the nationalists and the position of the authorities changed entirely. "The invasion of the schools by the Jews" was a slogan launched at an economic convention at Jassy in 1882 and it led many school principals to refuse the entry of Jewish pupils into their institutions.

In a circular of August 4, 1887, sent to the principals of elementary and secondary schools, the Minister of Public Education requested that if the number of registered pupils was too high, that priority be given to Romanians. Consequently, the percentage of Jewish children excluded from the public schools increased. After the failure of several initiatives, and in spite of the opposition of certain members of parliament and petitions sent to the Chamber and the Senate by the Jews, a new law on elementary schools was promulgated on June 4, 1892.

The most restrictive amendment to this law was adopted after a speech by A.C. Cuza, which began his long career as a professional anti-Semitic agitator. It started as follows:

> Elementary education is free and mandatory for Romanians.... Foreigners, except those living in Dobrudja, will pay a tax set by the regulation published in application of the present law. In exceptional cases, the Minister may grant a dispensation. If there is a shortage of spaces, preference will be given to the children of

Romanians. The school tax is set at 15 francs for rural schools and at 30 francs for city schools.

This law, which for the first time looked upon the Jewish children as foreigners, caused discontent not only among the Jewish population but even among certain Romanian Liberals. However, in spite of changes to the law in 1896, 1989, 1900, 1901, 1903 and 1904, it remained in force.

After eviction from the elementary schools, it was then the turn of secondary and higher schools. The law on secondary and higher education of April 4, 1898, provided in Article 2 that:

> Secondary and higher education is without charge for the sons of Romanians. The sons of foreigners may be admitted to the schools of different levels if spaces remain available, after applications by the sons of Romanians have been processed. In that case, they will pay a tax set by a rule for each school and payable to the school cashiers. The Minister can waive all or part of this tax for deserving or impoverished pupils.

The percentage of Jewish pupils in those schools was 11% in 1897/1898, but fell one year later to 7.5%.

The university field which was most accessible to Jews was medicine. In 1880, Jewish students represented 10.5% of the students in the School of Medicine in Bucharest and 28.6% in Jassy; in 1890, they comprised 31.5% and 41.3% of the student body, respectively; in 1893, 34.4% and 44.9%. In that last year, there were 200 Christian students in the Bucharest School of Medicine and 105 Jews; in Jassy, there were 56 Christians and 45 Jews. After 1899, an extremely high tax (360 francs) and the "lack of spaces" closed the door to many medical students.

Other laws excluded the Jews completely from the professional schools of agriculture and sylviculture, as well as from the teachers normal schools (Article 37 of the law on elementary education of 1896).

In the schools of Arts and Crafts (*Arts et Métiers*) and in the trade schools Jews could only be admitted as day pupils in a proportion of one to five, paying a high annual fee. The regulation pertaining to the higher schools of Arts and Crafts, dated May 21, 1906, contained the following provisions:

> Article 7 - Personnel engaged in practical training must be Romanians and only in case of need foreigners. Foreign master craftsmen are engaged by contract for a maximum of five years.
> Article 46 - Training in these schools is without cost for the sons of Romanians. They may be boarding students or day students.
> Article 47 - Foreigners may only be day students and pay an annual fee of 50 francs. The fee must be paid in full at the beginning of the year. Even the sons of those who obtained the rights of citizenship after the birth of their children will be considered foreigners. Other foreigners may only be admitted in the proportion of one fifth of the total number of vacant spaces and after the applications of the sons of Romanians have been processed.
> Article 119 - Foreigners may be admitted to this course in the order of their application, if there is space.

Thus, except for the schools to which entrance was entirely refused to Jews, the principle of *numerus clausus* was accepted and applied at all levels of the educational system.

Another aspect should be mentioned here to help in understanding the mental structures existing in the Romanian schools at the end of the nineteenth century: "the teaching of contempt." The Jewish students who were tolerated in the state schools had to suffer vexations stemming from collective indoctrination. Hatred and contempt of the Jews were often expressed by the teachers in the elementary schools and secondary schools right up to the universities. The teaching of contempt was also transmitted legally by the textbooks.

The logical consequence of the exclusion of Jewish children from the state schools was the creation of private Jewish schools by the Jewish communities across the country. However, since the government refused to give legal status to the Jewish communities, the existence of these private schools depended upon the generosity of the leaders. Many schools had only a brief existence, but by means of a school tax, private donations and, from the end of the century, through aid from the Jewish Colonization Association, the number of Jewish schools increased. According to statistics dating from 1912, there were in Romania 82 Jewish elementary schools of which 36 were subsidized by the J.C.A., 11 received financial assistance, and 26 were self-supporting. One school, established at Botosani in 1888, received constant help from the Universal Israelite Alliance.

Even these schools were the target of a series of humiliating regulations. A circular of October 21, 1899, prohibited the operation of Jewish schools on Sunday; another, dated April 17, 1900, compelled them to give instruction on Saturday. The latter also stipulated that instruction in Hebrew and religion might not last longer than two hours a day.

The whole series of laws and circulars in the field of education ended by largely attaining their objective - the debasement of Jewish youth.

The education laws, by encouraging and imposing ignorance, were only part of the overall policy of the authorities which aimed at eliminating the Jews from all branches of economic and liberal activity.

5. Laws on Liberal and Economic Professions

"The Moor has done his duty, now he can go." This expression represents the tactics of the lawmakers towards the Jews in the field of the liberal and economic professions. There was a relative tolerance as long as they were needed and a gradual exclusion as soon as they could be replaced or when they became bothersome. The most typical example was in medicine where the Jews had always played an important role.

The first law concerning the organization of the medical services was passed on June 20, 1874, and contained many discriminations against the Jews. They could not be appointed medical heads of the districts or hospitals, but could practice as physicians in the cities, as veterinarians and as midwives.

New pharmacies were only granted to Romanians and if there none available, then to foreigners (i.e., Jews) until 1878.

The medical law of April 3, 1885, stipulated:

Article 120 - No one may purchase the concession of a pharmacy unless he fulfills the conditions of Article 130 of this law.
Article 123, par. 3 - The concession of a pharmacy may only be given to Romanian pharmacists.
Article 128 - Permanent pharmacies must have the following staff: a responsible manager, at least one apprentice or a Romanian assistant. Only pharmacists who already have a Romanian apprentice have the right to receive foreign apprentices.
Article 131 - Pharmacists' aides, working under the direction of a head pharmacist, may be foreigners with a license in pharmacy, with the right of exercising their profession in the country.

Thus, tolerated at first, the Jews found themselves excluded and could be neither owners nor managers of a pharmacy.

Jews could not be appointed veterinary doctors in the cities or departments, under the regulations of July 24, 1894.

From November 13, 1896 on, Jewish physicians could not manage hospices.

The new medical law of December 20, 1910, specified that physicians, veterinary doctors, midwives, medical personnel, veterinary personnel, chemists, pharmacists, and nurses, in order to be admitted into these different services, must be Romanians or naturalized Romanians. If none are available, persons who do not enjoy Romanian nationality may be employed by contract for a limited time.

Even private hospitals, which were mostly religious foundations, did not accept Jewish physicians or Jewish midwives.

Along with medicine, another liberal career was closed to Jews: the law.

Despite a law of December 4, 1864, which provided that the profession of attorney could only be practiced by Romanians, Jews were authorized to plead before justices of the peace. This privilege was abolished in June 8, 1884, by Article 2 of a new law as follows: "All Romanians or naturalized Romanians, who pay for the appropriate license may practice the profession of attorney before justices of the peace, courts, appellate courts and the Supreme Court."

Jews were not excluded from the liberal professions alone: through the ingenious legislative machine, they were gradually removed from their usual occupations, trade and handicrafts. In the preceding period, Jews had begun to be excluded from commercial fields related to the status of civil servants. This was made clear by the law on the sale of tobacco of February 28, 1887, which stated that only Romanians or naturalized Romanians could be employed by the state monopoly (*régie*). This law affected not only many civil servants and wholesalers but also workers. It was carried out to the letter and all authorizations for the sale of tobacco were immediately withdrawn.

The law on alcoholic beverages of 1873 prohibited the Jews from such sale in the rural communities. This prohibition was lifted for a while during the Berlin Congress, but was reinstated in 1880. To reach the maximum number of people, Ion Bratianu sent out a circular on September 20, 1881, stating that small cities and towns be considered as belonging to rural communes. Two thousand families were hit by this measure as the occupation of tavern-keeper was closed to the Jews.

The law on stock exchanges dated July 16, 1881, whose purpose was to remove from the Jews the positions of exchange agents and brokers, opened the way for others in that field of business.

The most severe law was that relative to itinerant trade, dated March 29, 1884. Five thousand families who lived from trade as peddlers found their means of existence gone overnight and they were literally reduced the beggary. The June 25, 1884 edition of the newspaper *Bukarester Zeitung* published subscription lists and the names of aid committees set up to help them in different cities of the country.

The Zion Society in Bucharest turned to the large Jewish organizations in the West, the Alliance Israélite in Paris, one in Vienna, the Romanian Committee in Berlin and the Anglo-Jewish Association to obtain help for victims of that law. From a letter of November 17, 1884, sent by the president of that association, Adolphe Stern, we learn that through various subscriptions in the country, 1,600 persons were able to emigrate to Western Europe and America and that the emigration movement was intensifying.

The law on itinerant business was applied with great severity and serious abuses were committed. M. Panu, founder of the Radical Party, wrote in *Lupta* on August 19, 1884:

> I must admit that the law on itinerant business is being improperly applied. Under the pretext of itinerant trade, poor innocent people are being arrested; they are held at police stations until their file has been drawn up, as though this were a flagrant crime; then they are brought under escort before a justice of the peace; he convicts them at once and at the same time changes the fine to prison without even asking if they can pay; in the end, they are immediately put in jail.

Protests by the Jews were joined by those of Romanian merchants and workers who were deprived of their usual supplies. But in spite of this, the law was not repealed.

On May 13, 1886, a law was passed on the Chambers of Commerce and Industry which deprived the Jews - a large part of the merchants - of any decision in matters of business and industry.

Many other laws were passed eliminating the Jews from the customs service, from the hardware business, from tax collection in the communes, and from the railways. A climax was reached in 1902 in a law on the organization of trade which required in Article 4 that foreigners wishing to engage in a trade in Romania had to prove that equivalent rights were given to Romanians in their respective countries. Other articles in the same law excluded Jews from schools for adults giving instruction in the crafts, prohibited them from membership in corporation committees, and banned them from public adjudications.

The literal application of that law left the Jews with only one resort: mass emigration. Despite a statement by the government that Article 4 was not directed towards native Jews, great obstacles were placed in the way of the exercise of manual occupations. Later on, after numerous protests from abroad, Article 4 was amended in 1912 to exempt foreigners without other protection from that proof, but the other exclusions were not changed.

A regulation on the creation and administration of home industries in 1912 required Romanian nationality of pupils (girls) serving as apprentices in home industry shops.

A law of June 14, 1913, prohibited Jews from being brokers authorized by the Ministry of Industry and Commerce.

Among other discriminatory laws, let us note that Jews were excluded from the journalists' union (April 6, 1900).

During the same period, the Jews suffered the consequences of a harsh policy on expulsion.

6. Expulsions

During the trip of B. Boerescu throughout Europe to convince the Western cabinets that they should recognize Romanian independence, the policy of expulsions, which had calmed somewhat during the Berlin Congress, resumed actively. Following a ministerial despatch of July 24, 1879, Jews were arrested mainly in Bacau, Focsani, Vaslui, Falticeni and other towns in Moldavia and were then expelled under the pretext of vagrancy. A correspondent of the Israelite Alliance in Paris, J.M. Viertel, described in this way the expulsion of twenty-eight Jews of his city, most of whom were craftsmen:

> It was a poignant sight to see those poor people torn from their families of which they were the sole support. Women, becoming widows, their children orphans, made exclamations of despair which, unfortunately, could not keep the husbands and fathers which a ministerial order had banished! Among them there were some who were sick and were unable to make a trip on foot, but they were not allowed to go by car or railway. They protested in vain, for justice wanted it so. As their only consolation, they were given gendarmes who, as usual, treated the poor prisoners with all the weight of their soldiers' consideration....

This kind of arbitrary expulsion was ordered from April 18, 1881 on, through a law on *foreigners*.

Originally this law had been directed against Russian nihilists who found refuge in Romania after the assassination of Tsar Alexander II. It provided for the expulsion by decree of the Council of Ministers of *foreigners* who might disturb the peace or threaten national safety (Article 1). The government could expel anyone from the country without reason (Article 2). It was a terrible weapon and the government did not hesitate to use it improperly by applying it to the Jews. In 1885, on the basis of that law, the government decreed the banishment of several noted Jews who dared to criticize the arbitrariness of its policy of discrimination in the press. Among them were M. Gaster, a doctor of philosophy, decorated with the Order *Bene Merenti* for his books on Romanian language and literature; E. Schwartzfeld, a doctor of laws, editor-in-chief of the Jewish newspaper *Fraternitatea*, who had fought courageously against individual naturalization; J. Schein, who worked for the *Bukarester Freie Presse*; M. Aziel, editor-in-chief of the Yiddish daily *Hajoetz*; B. Brociner and I. Bettelheim of the *Bukarester Tagblatt*; and M. Rosenfeld and I.H. Fior of the *Vocea Dreptatii* of Botosani.

The expulsions extended from intellectuals to simple craftsmen and workers, to businessmen, rabbis and women. Certain Romanian members of parliament protested against the arbitrary nature of that law, but the law on foreigners was continued in force.

From 1880 to 1894, 859 persons were expelled from Romania. Of this number 163 were Jews. From 1894 to 1904, the total expelled rose to 6,529, of whom 1,177 were Jews.

Parallel to the expulsions from the country, the government continued its policy of expulsions from the villages. Many urban communes were changed for that purpose to rural communes.

In April, 1894, the Conservative minister Lascar Catargiu decided to expel from the rural communes of Moldavia families which had lived there for many decades. A delegation of Moldavian Jews ordered to leave their homes came to Bucharest and presented a moving petition. The King advised them to send a similar petition to the Chairman of the Council, but in spite of the King's intervention, Lascar Catargiu only agreed to postpone the planned expulsions for three weeks.

The policy of expulsions from the countryside intensified at the end of the nineteenth century and during the first decade of the twentieth.

All kinds of annoyances by the police took place in addition to these arbitrary and periodic expulsions.

Like genuine foreigners, the Jews were forced to obtain residence permits, identity papers and passports. Jews found without these papers (the administration created all sorts of difficulties in issuing them) were imprisoned and expelled as vagrants.

In 1887 the Romanian government succeeded in obtaining from Austria-Hungary the removal of the protection which the latter had given to some thousands of Jews and in this way almost all the Jews were subjected to Romanian laws as inhabitants of the country, as "foreigners not subject to foreign protection."

This deterioration in the status of the Jews from the standpoint of legislation found its roots in the ideological, nationalist and anti-Semitic platform which was clearly shown at the time of the Berlin Congress. The Jews had to suffer not only the consequences of the laws, the essential parts of which we have just presented, but also the repercussions of a growing anti-Semitic movement.

CHAPTER EIGHT

THE ANTI-SEMITIC MOVEMENT: IDEOLOGY AND MANIFESTATIONS

1. The Ideological Platform

Anti-Semitic Speeches in Parliament (1878-1879)

We have already discussed the elements in the rise of anti-Semitism prior to the Berlin Congress. These same elements showed themselves with even more strength in the following period and up to the First World War.

However, the years 1878-1879 must be considered a turning-point in the development of anti-Semitism in Romania. During the time between the Berlin Congress and the recognition of Romanian independence, the Jewish question held first place in the passionate debates of the legislature, in the press, and in political and literary publications.

The difference positions taken on the Jewish question reflect not only the nearly-unanimous desire to not grant emancipation of the Jews as provided in Article 44 of the Berlin Treaty, but they also indicate the growth of the anti-Semitic phenomenon which was entering upon a new phrase. New terms appeared in the language of the anti-Semitic nationalists; new grievances were added to earlier invectives and accusations. Many references to German and French ideologists constitute further proof of the internationalization of anti-Semitism. They prove that henceforth Romania was joining the European anti-Semitic movement.

In the speeches of the Romanian legislators, an important place is given to the myth of the Jews as a "state within the state." That slogan, which is frequently found in the classics of French anti-Semitism, entered Eastern Europe through the *Livre du Kahal* (1869), by the Russian apostate Jacob Brafman. The address by Senator Voinov in the session of March 10, 1879, is significant in showing the importance of the slogan "nation within the nation" in anti-Semitic language:

> It is immaterial in which country they live, the Jews do not become assimilated. They form a *nation within the nation* and remain immobile in a state of barbarism. You will find what I am

saying in a memorandum written in Russia by M. Brafman in which he notes the considerable influence of the Jews, their exclusiveness, the existence of a hidden government which they have formed in order to reach their objective.

The phrase "a state within the state" was used by other deputies in various speeches in which they defended the concept of a Christian state. Proposing naturalization on an individual basis, the deputy G. Misail ended on this note:

> Romania has been invaded. My only desire is this: when I am dead, let them inscribe on my tomb: "If he was wrong, it was with sincerity. All he wanted was for Romania to be always Christian, always Latin, beneath the sign of the Savior and the genius of eternal Rome."

The theory of the Christian state was also upheld by Deputy Vizenti, who attached it to the idea of nationality: "Since its creation and up to now this country has been an *entirely Christian country* and entirely Latin. This has been the great principle and the great feeling often joined to each other by which we have always defended *our nationality* and our patrimony."

For the first time, the racial question was raised. During the session of March 10, 1879, Senator Voinov quoted the Marquis of Pepoli, who defended Romania in the Italian Senate. The Marquis said: "In Romania the Jewish question is a racial question. It is not true that the Jews who live in Romania are Romanians; they belong to a race which has superimposed itself on the Romanian people."

The theory of race as foundation of the state was also defended by Deputy Magheru, who later offered a new text for Article 7: "To be well-organized, a state should have inhabitants of a single race or take the appropriate measures to create a homogenous climate."

Finally, let us note that Titu Maiorescu, an influential member of the Conservative Party, and leader of the literary group *Junimea*, while also stressing the importance of race and that the Romanians belonged to the Latin race, called for removal of the religious discrimination contained in Article 7. He said:

We who are a constitutional state of modern
form, established after the Oriental war by the
Treaty of Paris, due particularly to the insistence
of generous France, a member of our Latin race,
we were not created because we are the Orthodox
of the East, but because we are the advance sentinel of the Latin race in the Orient, like an oasis
in the desert of other races.... So why are you
placing in the constitution of this Latin race in the
Orient an exclusion by reason of religion? Despite
your fears, you cannot establish a religious
restriction.

A new grievance was expressed by Deputy Leca - the Jews
foment revolution:

They will corrupt our people; they will introduce
the commune as in the other countries, because
they are the leaders of the communists. You will
recall that, as French citizens, in the army during
the siege of Paris, instead of fighting the enemy,
they provoked civil war, they set fire to Paris.
Who did that? The co-religionists of those who
now want to insert themselves into the Romanian
community.

The poet Vasile Alecsandri was the only one in all the sections
of the Senate to oppose the revision of Article 7 in any form whatsoever. In his address at the Senate session of October 22, 1879, after
the new Article 7 had been approved by the Chamber, he again
denounced the danger of the "Jewish invasion" and declared that the
best support of the "invaders" came from Freemasonry and gold.

What is this new ordeal, this new invasion? Who
are the invaders? Whence do they come? What do
they want? And who is the new Moses who is
leading them to the Promised Land, situated this
time on the banks of the Danube? Who are these
invaders? They are an active people, intelligent,
indefatigable in accomplishing their mission. They

are followers of the blindest religious fanaticism, the most exclusive of all the inhabitants of the earth, the least capable of assimilation to the other peoples of the world! ...Faithful to their religion until death, their leaders are the rabbis who lay down special laws for them; their homeland is the Talmud! Their power is enormous, for two other powers form their base and their support: religious Freemasonry and gold.

The Pamphlets of I. Slavici and D. Rossetti-Tetcanu

Most of the accusations made in the parliamentary debates which we have cited are found in two extremely violent anti-Semitic pamphlets published in 1879: *"Soll" and "Haben": The Jewish Question in Romania*, by Ioan Slavici, and *Romania and the Jews Before Europe*, by Deputy D. Rossetti-Tetcanu. The first was written in Romanian and the second in French, translated by the philosopher V. Conta, who will be mentioned later. The purpose of these two pamphlets was to convince the Romanian parliament and Europe respectively of the validity of the thesis of not granting political emancipation to the Jews.

In his pseudo-social study, Ioan Slavici, of Transylvania, denounced the Jewish invasion and criticized the corrupt character of the Jews who formed, "a social disease of which no nation can rid itself." Because of them, he wrote, the ills of the country are growing day by day. The solution would be to expel them, but no one wants to receive them. "All that remains for us is to close the borders at a certain time, and kill them, throw them all into the Danube, so that no seed of theirs remains! According to all sound reason, that is the only way out for our tenacious nation under present circumstances." On this macabre and prophetic note Slavici anticipated the "final solution".

The same tocsin and the same accusations echo in the pamphlet by Rossetti-Tetcanu, who wrote: "The Jew is an unhealthy germ, a bearer of epidemics. Whenever the Occident is sick and takes an emetic, it looks at Moldavia and regurgitates the Jew in torrents. Yes, you may be sure, you elect of God: you are a social virus."

The classic religious grievance was as follows: "It was not for nothing that a Jew betrayed Christ: that was a great example and a great warning. Be on your guard, O you nations which let yourselves be lulled to sleep by Mosaic flattery! Romanians, Judas is preparing to embrace you. Lift your eyes to the bleeding body of Him Who was crucified!"

The racial grievance and the "slogan a state within a state" was presented thus:

> Just as everywhere it [the Jewish race] has formed a separate class and has stood out in the itinerant trade in Romania, its separatist tendency has been extremely marked. It is not a race capable of blending with another. It is not capable of assimilation. A state within a state with its king, its ministers, its administration, its laws, its wealth and its constitution.

However, the main argument was that of preserving the nationality and the author, among absurd accusations, declared: "No one more than us would applaud the resurrection of Jewish nationality. The Jews in Palestine, the Romanians in Romania. That is geography for everyone."

These two pamphlets reveal the depth of anti-Semitic feeling in their authors whose nationalism was aggravated by Article 44 of the Berlin Treaty. However, they only had a minor influence on public opinion which, though hostile to the Jews, did not favor such extreme solutions. On the other hand, Vasile Conta and Mihail Eminescu, who were more subtle, and particularly A.C. Cuza, among others, contributed to a genuine ideological platform.

The Theoreticians: V. Conta, M. Eminescu, A.C. Cuza

The philosopher Vasile Conta (1845-1882), a former Professor of Law at the University of Jassy who was minister for a time, wrote several important books: *The Theory of Fatalism* (1875-1876), *The Theory of Universal Undulation* (1876-1877), *The Origin of Species* (1877) and *An Essay on Metaphysics* (1879). Through his materialistic and atheistic ideas, he prepared the way for the future penetration of Marxist thought in Romania. He was also a bitter enemy of the Jews and his thinking is reflected in a famous speech made before the Chamber on September 5, 1879, in which he opposed the granting of political rights. He placed the principle of national conservation above those of liberty and equality and declared that declared that "if we do not struggle against the Jewish element, we shall perish as a nation." His grievances, polarized on the economic and national aspect, may be reduced to this sentence, to use a modern expression: Romanian nationality is being polluted by the Jews. Petre Carp referred to him as "the man who has collected all the mud of the accusations against the Jews and threw it at the Romanian parliament."

Vasile Conta extended the fight he had waged before the Chamber by creating an anti-Semitic association known as *Viata* ("Life"), which lasted for only a short time, where he called for a permanent secret struggle. This was his swan song on the Jewish question.

A thorough study of Eminescu and the Jews has still to be done. His attitude was often ambiguous and the anti-Semitism of his polemical writings should be looked upon more as an important component of his nationalistic ideology, but not as an instinctive atavistic reaction. In the little-known publication *Curierul de Iasi* of which he was for a time one of the editors, Eminescu expressed himself several times on the Jewish question. On September 29, 1876, he took umbrage at the ill treatment inflicted of the Jews in an article entitled "Against the Ill Treatment Inflicted on the Jews." On the other hand, in the most important article dated January 9, 1877, entitled "The Jews and the Conference," he took a hostile stand and came out in opposition to the granting of political rights to the Jews, saying that they were incapable of "sacrifice and work." The Jew, he said, cannot love the country where he lives, because with him the feeling of race is too strong. The Jews are different from the Romanian nation, they speak another language and represent a weapon for foreigners against Romania. Finally, they have created their own Internationale, the Israelite Alliance, which has branches in every country with the sole purpose of maintaining constant tension under the pretext of oppression. After the Berlin Congress, Eminescu published his main critical articles: "The Jewish Question: I. Usury; II. The Results of Usury in Romania; III. Industry and Trade; IV. The Regulation of Relations with the Jews in Prussia; V. The Israelite Alliance."

Insofar as the Jews were productive, as in the case of craftsmen, Eminescu was ready to accept them. While opposing political emancipation, he made a distinction within Jewry, pointing out that some are useful and beneficial to the country, especially the "Spanish Jews":

> We are sorry for them which are relatively few in number, even though there are from 2,000 to 3,000 of them in our country; we are sorry for the "Spanish Jews," who have nothing in common with the "Polish Jews," but everyone can understand that in a foreign army which is coming to us, no one will try to seek the difference in the limited number of friends who may be part of that army. And the Jews are an economical army.

Then he expresses his apprehension over the masses of the Jews, of whom he exaggerated the number at 600,000.

In reality, Eminescu added nothing new to the well-known accusations and grievances, but, different from the other nationalists, he thought that the Jewish question ought to be solved in a constructive way, through integration of the Jews.

In an unpublished note after the Berlin Congress, he wrote that unfortunately no one in the country had the courage to suggest the only equitable solution, namely, "to treat the foreigners (Jews) as equals, completely erasing at the same time any religious distinctions."

Eminescu was much more severe towards the Greeks, Bulgars, Armenians and other Christian minorities who had infiltrated the "national" bourgeoisie. He said, for example, that the Jew was as cunning as the Greek, but less corrupt. "The Jews are ten times more honest, more moral and more humane than those people."

Eminescu played an important role in Romanian nationalism and it may be said his anti-Semitism was taken up by A.C. Cuza, his anti-democratism by Aurel Popovici, his populism by Nicolae Iorga and his racial theories by Vasile Parvan. The sociologist Stefan Zeletin said that he was the greatest figure in the Romanian reaction against the middle class.

Mihail Eminescu belonged to the *Junimea* group, a Conservative literary association whose members included the best representatives of the country's intellectual elite in the last third of the nineteenth century. It publication was the review *Convorbiri literare* (Literary Conversations). It was Eminescu's thinking that there was disagreement between the modern political form and the real content of Romanian society; this idea was likewise supported by the Junimists. Placing the social value of the peasant above all, the Junimists were opposed to technology, urbanism and bourgeois civilization. They were opposed to the Jews, because they were an important element in the cities, playing an economic role in them which this group wanted to abolish by any means possible.

However certain Junimist leaders like Titu Maiorescu and Petre Carp opposed religious discrimination and advocated the assimilation of the Jews. In 1879, they proposed granting civic rights to certain categories of Jews.

At the beginning of the twentieth century, two new literary currents took up the Junimist ideas and carried them further. The leader of the first school was the historian Nicolae Iorga (1871-1940) who opposed change in the old social structures and demanded a return to the past which his group idealized. The second, headed by the philosopher Constantin Stere, proposed a plan for a new society in which every peasant would become the owner of a small farm in a "peasant democracy." According to Stere, the development of big industry was incompatible with the Romanian soul, so he called for only the development of handicraft industries. As a professor at the University of Jassy and a parliamentary deputy, he published a controversial study, entitled "Social Democracy or Populism," in which he declared his opposition to industrial society of the Western type with its inevitable consequences: owners and workers, capitalists and proletariat, doctrinaire or revolutionary socialism. He also touched on the Jewish problem and suggested that the state aid the Jews to emigrate. This, according to him, was the only solution in view of their demographic growth.

The economists Petre Aurelian and A.D. Xenopol took similar positions, but in a different way. The first was the author of *A Catechism of Political Economy* in which he called for improvement in the condition of the peasants, the decentralization of industry in the countryside and a strict economic protectionism. He played an important role in the Liberal Party and when he became a minister, put forward harsh measures against Jewish craftsmen and businessmen in 1900 and 1901.

A.D. Xenopol, known primarily as an historian, collected part of his economic studies in a volume entitled *Studii economice* (1879). There he called for a native industry encouraged by the state. But he also did not believe in the development of big industry and wrote in 1895 that: "Romania will never become an industrial country in the true meaning of the word.... There is only one way for us to follow if we do not want to die, that of introducing into our country branches of industry attached to agriculture, of creating agricultural industries everywhere." The son of a Greek mother and a Jewish father converted to the Orthodox Christian religion, A.D. Xenopol was hostile to the Jews for economic as well as religious reasons. He felt that the conversion of the Jews was the best way to bring about assimilation.

Finally, let us mention especially Alexandru C. Cuza (1858-1944), who was the most illustrious anti-Semitic agitator of the twentieth century, beginning his political activity at the beginning of the century. Whereas Aurelian and Xenopol and others militated from the start for complete nationalism, Cuza began his political career as a socialist and atheist. In 1883 he was at Brussels in the socialist circle of Mille Badarau, who edited the magazine *Dacia viitoare* ("The Future Dacia"). He quickly changed his thinking on contact with the *Junimea* Society and substituted a conservative nationalism for his socialism.

Before being appointed Professor of Political Economy at the University of Jassy, he published in 1893 a study entitled *The Romanian Artisan* in which he showed himself to be a fierce supporter of economic protectionism and proposed new laws of exception against the Jews. He repeated the old refrain that the Jews could not be assimilated, that they exploited and corrupted Romanian business:

> Without using unusual means of defense, no nation has been able to resist the competition of this band which is expressly organized to exploit those who do not belong to their group. A businessman or an artisan can easily hold out against another artisan or businessman, but when faced by an infamous coalition which purposely manipulates prices to live from the sale of the lowest quality of merchandise, honest trade must give way.

In 1899, A.C. Cuza published with another Junimist the newspaper *Era noua* (The New Era) which included articles influenced by certain ideas of Eminescu. His anti-Semitic nationalism was expressed in a book *Despre poporatie* (On the Population). Its themes were not new and much space was given to his concern with the growth of the Jewish population on one hand and the shrinking of the Christian population on the other. He outlined this view in a later article called "The Nationalization of the Trades", published in 1902 at the time of the famous law on the trades.

To eliminate the Jews from economic positions, he called for the government to intervene with laws aimed at protecting "national labor." He expressed his desire to push the struggle as far as possible and stated in his conclusion:

> Either we, as Romanians, shall succeed in re-conquering the ground lost in trade and industry, reestablishing the national middle class so that it may absorb the overflow from the villages and support the managerial classes, and then we shall live as a nation existing by itself with our own, Romanian culture, with our patrimony, or else the Jews will continue to take hold of trade and industry, conquering our cities and ending up by crushing us and then they will make up the foreign middle class.

The cycle of articles "*Nationalitatea in arta*," published in the review *Fat-Frumos* at Barlad and later collected in one volume in 1906, represents an attempt at defining the national spirit in art. For Cuza, the only aesthetic criterion was that of blood, the artist's ethnic origin. Racial purity was the only guarantee of the value of an artistic or literary work. In German literature, Heine's work seemed to him to lack any aesthetic criterion. Likewise, in the Danubian area, the only creators of the beautiful could only be "men of the blood." In this theoretical collection, *Nationality in Art*, the author displays extremist chauvinism, a frenzied xenophobia and his writing is considered the most violent and reactionary among those which appeared in current publications.

Cuza's anti-Semitic political activity found new expression from 1907 on through his contributions to *Neamul romanesc* (The Romanian Nation), founded by N. Iorga in 1906. Elected Deputy in 1911 by the Second College at Jassy, A.C. Cuza was present in the Romanian parliament until 1938. It is he who chose the swastika as a symbol of the Christian nationalist movement. In his hatred of the Jews, he denied that they had made any contribution to civilization and he proposed that the Old Testament not be recognized by the Orthodox Church.

There is no doubt that there was a correlation between his instinctive, morbid hatred of the Jews - not including Jewish women - and certain profound deformations in his personality. In 1923, he launched this warning: "Leave the country while there is still time in order not to be drowned in blood. Before my death, I should like to see the blood of the Jews mingled with the mud." Careful analysis of his neurotic attitudes would not only be enlightening in understanding his morbid fantasies, but also especially in understanding the psychosis which affected the Iron Guard. But all of that lies outside the chronological framework of the present study.

2. Anti-Semitic Organizations

The doctrine of anti-Semitism which was carved out at the time of the Berlin Congress did not remain in the hands of the elite; it grew rapidly in various milieus conditioned by the "teaching of scorn" and through emotional underground currents which created a stereotype: the negative image of the Jew.

Many clergymen, army officers, civil servants, public school teachers, professors and students formed the framework of the anti-Semitic movement in the closing decades of the nineteenth and the beginning of the twentieth centuries. What were the manifestations of the movement?

First, there were groups, associations, and clubs whose members came from different professions with the stated slogan of fighting the Jews on the economic ground and organizing a systematic boycotting against them. The cooperative movement and all the economic conventions took as their slogan: "Not a needle for the Jews!" The policy of boycotting was encouraged by official representatives of the Orthodox Church, who accused the Jews of being the principal cause of the estrangement of Romanians from their religion. The anti-Semites constantly placed their economic programs under the sign of the cross. This shows the convergence of material interests with centuries-old religious prejudices. In fact, the anti-Semites used these prejudices to remove the Jews from their economic positions.

The Romanian-European Anti-Semitic Convention of 1886

The Romanian-European Anti-Semitic Convention held in Bucharest from September 7 to 9, 1886, was an important moment in the history of the anti-Semitic movement. The Universal Anti-Israelite Alliance was created in that year. Its president was the Liberal senator Edouard Ghergel, while other leading Romanian anti-Semites included Moriu, a former captain, and Butculescu, a senator, member of the Liberal Party and editor of the newspaper *Desteptarea* (Awakening).

The government of Ion Bratianu placed the Athénée Hall at the disposition of the anti-Semites free of charge and on that occasion the government publications *Vointa nationala* (The National Will) and *Steaua romana* (The Romanian Star) wrote violent anti-Jewish articles and complimented the members of the convention. The latter promised to propagate and execute the following:

(1) The Jews are recognized as being unworthy of remaining any longer in Europe among the nations.

(2) Until a way is found to expel them from the European countries, the congress asks its members from Romania, France, Hungary and all other countries which adhere to its decisions to ask their governments and legislatures:

(a) Not to grant from the nation, districts or communes any concession to the Jews, in any form, even as a loan;

(b) Not to grant any position with a salary paid by the nation, district or commune to any Jew, including insurance companies, banks, etc.;

(c) Not to sell any property to Jews, not to allow them to cultivate land, build houses or operate mills (likewise, no one is to lease land, houses, hotels or cabarets to Jews);

(d) To prohibit Jews from operating establishments such as restaurants, hotels, cafés, breweries, distilleries and wine shops and prevent them from being bakers, grocers, grain merchants, physicians and pharmacists;

(e) To ask clergymen of all faiths to propagate these ideas among their parishioners, and teachers in their schools, in order that they purchase nothing from Jews and employ none in their service;

(f) All nations which adhere to these decisions should urge their governments to pass legislation in this direction and form committees to ask for application of these decisions through collective petitions.

A second convention was held on September 12 in Craiova, the capital of Oltenia in Wallachia, which was attended by 2,000 persons. At the end of the meeting, the crowd, which had been excited by the speakers and led by a priest E. Petrescu, attacked the Jewish quarter.

A trip to Moldavia by Jacques de Biez and divers other Romanian anti-Semites caused similar disturbances. In 1887, L'Alliance Anti-Israelite Universelle published the *Archives anti-israelites*, which did not last long, and another group, the Société Antisemitique Roumaine, published a newsletter entitled *L'Anti-semite*.

At the close of the nineteenth century anti-Semitic committees were organized in most of the provincial towns, especially in Moldavia, where the most active one was that of Barlad. Prior to elections the anti-Semitic committee published a manifesto of the so-called "National Anti-Semitic Party." It contained the well-known slogans of expulsion of the Jews from the countryside, refusal to rent land to them, excluding them from the army and restrictive laws called laws of "national defense."

The Anti-Semitic Alliance (1895)

The Anti-Semitic Alliance was founded in Bucharest in 1895 by Nae Dumitrescu, a lycée professor who also held an important position in the Ministry of National Education. This alliance included a considerable number of politicians and government employees.

Among the latter was the Minister of Public Education, I. Istrati, who created the anti-Semitic newspaper *Apararea Nationala* (National Defense) which appeared from 1900 to 1903.

Among the most significant of the by-laws of this alliance let us note the following:

Chapter I. Today, November 8, 1895, the Anti-Semitic Alliance was established in Bucharest, with branches throughout the country and relations with all foreign associations which followed the same objective.

The Alliance is essentially economic and has the following purpose:

(a) The struggle by all means allowed and is all directions to preserve the Romanian element against the Jewish element;

(b) To protect and develop Romanian trade in the hands of Romanians;

(c) To encourage Romanian trade by Romanians and reduce the financial influence which the Jews have acquired;

(d) To struggle against Jewish usury and speculation in all branches of agriculture, particularly in Moldavia;

(e) To preserve and develop religious feeling and struggle against the corrupting action of the Jews and the demoralization caused by an erroneous interpretation of humanitarian principles;

(f) To encourage and protect the Romanian workers;

(g) As the Jewish element cannot be assimilated, the Alliance will fight against increasing the political rights to be granted the Jews;

(h) It will employ all means allowed to make it impossible for Jews in Romania and support their emigration from the country.

In order to reach this goal with greater security, the Alliance will be a secret society. Upon admission, each member will take an oath to maintain secrecy concerning all transactions and aims of the Alliance, as well as the names its members, and that he will devote all his knowledge and energy to defending the good cause.

Chapter II. The Alliance will disseminate anti-Semitic principles in Romania through newspapers, conferences, brochures, etc.; in addition, it will take measures to paralyze the influence of the Jews in the area of credit, the press, trade and property.

Chapter IV. To insure unity of direction in the interests of the Alliance, central and supreme power is placed in a council named the Grand Anti-Semite Council, with its headquarters at Bucharest.

Chapter V. Any Christian Romanian may become a member by making the appropriate application.

To become a member of the Alliance, the following conditions must be met: (1) Be at least 21 years old; (2) have honorable employment; (3) Agree to anti-Semitic principles; and (4) have a good reputation.

Chapter VI. Income of the Alliance stems from registration fees, dues and gifts, the sale of insignia, diplomas, membership cards, payments, receipts from balls, conferences, lotteries, concerts, etc.

Every year there will be an anti-Semite congress at Bucharest for which the Grand Council will set the agenda two weeks in advance.

Every Romanian who makes a gift of 100 to 500 francs will be entitled to wear the insignia of the "Order of Anti-Semite Knight" (*Cavaler Antisemit*).

Anyone who make a gift of 500 to 1,000 francs will be entitled to wear the insignia of the "Order of Saint Michael", the patron of the Alliance.

One year after his admission, each member will receive a diploma as anti-Semite, if the Grand

Council finds that such member has fulfilled all the duties demanded of him and has struggled energetically to accomplish the duties assigned to him by the Alliance, and he has paid a fee of 10 francs for the diploma.

All members who have the anti-Semite diploma and who have distinguished themselves in the mission entrusted to them by the Alliance may obtain the "Order of the Cross."

Members who have the order of the "Cross" may obtain successively the "Order of Anti-Semite Knight" and that of "Saint Michael" if they have been found worthy of them by a vote of the Grand Council for service rendered to the Alliance.

The Alliance will work in relation with and in agreement with foreign anti-Semitic alliances.

The Alliance will have its own printing press.

The Grand Council and each section will have their own special flag.

These by-laws, of which only part are given here, are similar to those of Freemasonry.

What is striking in reading these by-laws as also in the programs of the other anti-Semitic organizations, the most important of which was the Anti-Semitic League (*Ligue Antisémite*) were not only the accusations and the determination "to make the situation of the Jews impossible in Romania" through a complete and systematic boycotting, but also the stress laid on the ties with anti-Semites of other countries. On the one hand, this affirmed complete nationalism and on the other, the supranational nature of these organizations. This was not limited to Romania, and Hannah Arendt, in her book *Sur l'Antisémitisme*, stated, while placing this phenomenon on a political plane, that in the West "the aim of the anti-Semites was not the conquest of power in a single country, but an inter-European government above all nations."

In contrast with Western anti-Semites for whom the struggle against the Jews meant also a struggle against the State which symbolized their protection and success, in Romania, instead, the anti-Semites held to the view of a *national State* and accused the Jews

of being an occult force which sought to gnaw away at its foundations. The relentlessness of the anti-Semites in not granting political
rights to the Jews resulted from that fear. In a society contaminated
by the anti-Semitic virus, in which the two historical parties compete
with each other in legislating against the Jews, these organizations
came to be used as pressure groups, particularly at the time of
electoral campaigns. They played an active role in the brutal persecutions which took place from time to time in different cities, the
most sadly famous being the disorders in December, 1897, in
Bucharest and in May, 1899, in Jassy.

The Disturbances of 1897 and 1899

In Bucharest disturbances broke out following a draft law by
General Berindei intended to exclude Jews from the army. This
caused lively agitation among the Jewish reservists. The latter held a
meeting to protest this draft law and nationalist students answered by
an anti-Jewish meeting at the close of which bands singing the
patriotic anti-Semitic hymn "Desteapta-te Romane!" (Wake up,
Romania!) ran through the Jewish quarter and pillaged Jewish
synagogues, stores and houses. The rioters, armed with cudgels and
iron bars worked under the benevolent eyes of the police who only
went into action at the end of the riot. When the disturbance had
ended, ministers and consuls representing the foreign powers visited
the devastated streets to see what had happened. Through their dean,
M. Fontin, the Russian Minister, expressed to the President of the
Council their regret at the inertia of the police.

During the session of the Senate on December 7, Petre Carp
refuted the allegations by Minister of the Interior Pherekyde, who
had said the Jews were responsible for the excesses which had been
committed and in his conclusion he traced the following portrait of
the situation of the Jews:

> ...The Minister tells us that this kind of movement
> is also taking place elsewhere and that anti-
> Semitism is almost an European movement. That
> may well be, but then I shall ask you: would anti-
> Semites cause similar disturbances in France, in
> Germany, in Austria, if Jews were in the same
> situation there as they are here? Obviously not. In
> those countries Jews enjoy full rights, while they

do not have any here. There only remained one thing for them, the individual hope that by means of an undeniable sacrifice, of which Horace said *Dulce et decorum est pro patria mori*, they might also become citizens. Well! Through General Berindei's law you are today destroying the only hope of that population which has no rights. From now on, it can no longer hope to find in our country, not only as a group, but even as individuals, a homeland which it does not have. You speak of foreigners, but are these foreigners subjects from abroad or are they Romanian subjects? They are Romanian subjects, they do not enjoy the protection of another country and you yourselves are not allowing them the natural protection of our nation and so we find ourselves in the presence of a population of 300,000 persons who are outside the law, not protected either by us or by the government of another country, because they do not belong to another country. And are you not aware of the hatred which is slowly growing over generations in the heart of that population? Do you not realize that, instead of attenuating little by little the antagonism between the Christian and Jewish populations, you are only inflaming it? You are only creating lightheartedly within your country bitter and numerous enemies and I shall repeat that you will not be able to get rid of them.

In the end, the Berindei draft law was not taken into consideration, but anti-Semitic agitation continued to spread throughout the country. The disturbances of May 28, 1899, which took place in Jassy were brought about by the National Students' Committee which distributed a violent anti-Semitic manifesto in the city which called upon the population to unite and make decisions to defend "Romanianism." After that meeting, during which the crowd was excited by incendiary speeches among which were those made by two women, Elena Sevastos of Jassy and Tita Pavelescu of Focsani, the same scenes of pillage occurred as had taken place in Bucharest two years before.

The Anti-Semitic League grew rapidly and took root in nearly all the cities, causing many acts of violence. The following petition made to King Carol by members of the Jewish community of Roman on August 6, 1900, illustrates the dangers to which all the Jews were exposed:

> Sire, since measures were announced today aimed at preventing Jews from emigrating, we are taking the liberty in all humility to approach the Throne. The Anti-Semitic League is persecuting us to death. Wherever this League exists - and it exists in most of the cities and towns - it represents nothing but suffering and misery for us. Here at Roman they are acting in a way that shows the cruelty of Christians can exceed all limits. At the head of the League are the mayor and Senator J. Balensti, the commander of the garrison E. Garceanu, the director of the post and telegraph and other government officials and judges. It is easy for these gentlemen to stir up hundreds of persons against us, including many vagabonds who attack us from time to time like wild beasts, committing the most violent acts of cruelty. For this reason we beg Your Majesty to take pity on us and to help us, so that, if we are reduced to poverty, we may at least have our lives protected in our misery. O Majesty, remove us from the hands of these bloody people. What have we done? Nothing except to have been born in this country. We are doing no harm to anyone. We only want to work in order to live under the protection of the laws.

Along with the anti-Semitic organizations, there arose a number of newspapers - generally of short duration - expressing their hatred of the Jews between 1892 and 1906.

The Nationalist-Democratic Party (1910)

The newspaper *Neamul romanesc* was founded in 1906 by the historian Nicolae Iorga (1871-1940). Iorga was a nationalist who was quick to take offense and between the two wars he played an important role in politics as Minister and President of the Council. At the beginning of the twentieth century he was a partisan and propagator of anti-Semitic ideas. Later, his opinions changed radically and he suffered a tragic death, assassinated in especially unpleasant circumstances by fascists of the Iron Guard, but before the First World War he constantly denounced the "Jewish peril" in both his historical writings and in the press.

In *Neamul romanesc* he used a permanent subtitle "The Peasant Question and Our Jews" and through his readers who were priests and school teachers, he propagated the venom of hatred among the peasant masses. His campaigns greatly aided the anti-Semite movement at the start of the peasant revolt in 1907.

During that revolt, the anti-Semitic nationalists came together and tried to give a political expression to their aspirations. In November, 1907, after the revolt, there was a large meeting in Jassy of the nationalists who were anti-Semitic where Nicolae Iorga and A.C. Cuza took part. The speeches given contained all the grievances of the anti-Semites of which Piat, the French Consul in Jassy, gave us all the small details.

The meetings of A.C. Cuza and N. Iorga did not take concrete form until 1910 through the creation of the Nationalist-Democratic Party, the first political party whose program centered solely on anti-Semitic policy.

The essential part of that program was expressed by A.C. Cuza in the "five theses" which contained "the nationalist solution of the Jewish problem:"

> 1) The Jewish problem is an organic one which the Romanian people are called upon to resolve by conscience, work and economy and the solution of which can only be the elimination of the Jews, their gradual replacement in all the branches of activity which they have seized by surprise while we were not ready in our territory over which we alone have ethnic and historical rights of possession.

2) Any government called upon to lead Romania
has the duty of helping the nation represented by
our State - and it alone is and can be represented
by this State - in its efforts at solving the Jewish
problem. And the means by which it may be
solved have been clearly formulated in the
nationalist program.
They are:
    - protection and stimulation of Romanian ef-
forts;
    - creation of cooperative associations;
    - allocation of equipment and public businesses
to Romanian craftsmen and businessmen;
    - expulsion of the Jews from the countryside
where they have no right to live;
    - exclusion of Jews from the army;
    - elimination of Jews from the Romanian
press;
    - exclusion of the Jews from all Civil Service;
    -strict application of the law on encouragement
of industry insofar as Romanian personnel are
concerned.
3) In Romania no one has the right to engage in
politics concerning us, our country's interests, or
the future of this country except Romanians.
Freedom of the press and of association are rights
guaranteed by the constitution exclusively to
Romanian citizens.
4) Discussions of the Jews by Jews cannot be
tolerated. For, if they are naturalized citizens,
they have nothing more to demand and if they are
not, as foreigners, they have no right to debate.
5) The Romanian people and each of its governments must abide by Article 7 as modified and no
party in Romania can lower itself by offering
more than that. Thus the Jewish agitation is
entirely useless and dangerous for them, provok-
ing the legitimate resentment of the Romanian
people. For the Jews there remains the legal way
of naturalization as individuals and their machi-

nations outside the law must be repressed by each government in the interest of public order.

As we see, this extremist program aimed at eliminating the Jews from all areas of social, economic, military, cultural and political life.

The new party had its foundation among the clergy, the teachers, students and governmental civil servants.

One year after the foundation of the Nationalist-Democratic Party, Nicolae Iorga was elected a member of the Romanian Academy. Enjoying increased prestige, he also headed the Popular University of Valenii de munte, which has been transformed into a center for anti-Semitic propaganda, particularly in the courses of A.C. Cuza. The influence of the two professors expanded into wider spheres and they were supported by the powerful Cultural League for the Union of All Romanians (an irredentist organization claiming the return of Transylvania, Bukovina and Bessarabia to the "mother-country"). However, the Nationalist-Democrats did not gain much ground and did not become a great party.

The extent of anti-Semitic feeling, on the one hand, and the openly anti-Semitic policies of the Liberals and the Conservatives on the other, explain why the Nationalist Democratic Party and the leagues and organizations described above were unable to play a role, at least until the First World War, other than a secondary one.

Conversely, through their clever propaganda, anti-Semitism, which from 1878 had been primarily an urban phenomenon, won over in the first decade of the twentieth century part of the peasant masses who were convinced by clever agitators that the cause of their great poverty emanated from the Jews.

On August 5, 1900, Take Ionescu wrote to A. Henry, the French Ambassador in Bucharest, that "in our country the issues which create ministries or cause them to fall only interest a few hundred politicians and leave the rest of the nation indifferent; the only question which is capable of exciting them is the Jewish question. Romanians would prefer making common cause with Russia than agreeing to equality and sharing sovereignty with the Jews." The same ambassador wrote to his Minister of Foreign Affairs: "Anti-Semitism is more than an opinion in Romania. It is a passion where politicians of all parties come together, the represen-

tatives of Orthodoxy and, one may add, all the Wallachian and
Moldavian peasants."

3. The Peasant Revolt of 1907

The peasant rising in the spring of 1907 constituted a tragic
episode for the Romanian Jews. The peasant revolt, the essential
cause of which was their great poverty, represents by its extent and
duration the most important popular insurrection in the history of
Romania.

It broke out in a village of northern Moldavia which bore the
significant name of *Flaminzi* ("the starving ones"), spread to neighboring districts, turned south and reached its maximum of violence
in Wallachia in the districts of Vlasca, Teleorman, Olt and Dolj. The
beginning of the uprising was clearly anti-Semitic and a recent
publication by Karl Scheerer notes that the Jews were the first
victims. In this rising, the Jewish question was a catalyst revealing
social tensions: whereas in the beginning, the anger of the peasants
was directed against Jewish farmers - in fact many small businessmen, shopkeepers, craftsmen and workers who were Jews were
ruined - it quickly changed orientation and the rioters turned against
those who were really responsible, the large landowners. The
greatest devastation took place in areas containing few or no Jews
(Wallachia and its western section, Oltenia).

To crush the revolt, the Liberal government which had taken
the place of the Conservatives employed the army which waged real
"battles" using artillery to level entire villages: close to 11,000
peasants were killed.

The anti-Jewish orientation of the start of the revolt was due to
the unjustified measures of exception (i.e., laws, expulsions) taken by
the authorities against the Jews on the one hand, and the large
number of incendiary articles published by the teachers and the
priests on the other.

There were 27 localities where the Jews suffered particularly
and in certain ones, besides 47 killed or wounded, the losses were
considerable.

The Jewish Alliance in Paris received many letters of distress
requesting financial aid. Aid committees were formed in the principal cities. One of the appeals of this kind from Jassy ran as follows:

All mankind is deeply impressed by the recent
bloody riots which have occurred in many cities
and towns of the country, resulting in the deaths
of thousands of people of all social strata, especially the poor. The few goods belonging to the
latter have been scattered; the merchandise of the
small businessmen and the working tools of the
modest craftsmen and workers have been
destroyed, and those who escaped the murderous
attacks and violence remain without resources,
even lacking daily sustenance.

Written in German, this appeal was signed by Rabbi I. Niemerower
and Dr. Karpel Lippe.

The Jewish Alliance in Paris launched a subscription which
was widely answered even by small communities such as Djelfa in
southern Algeria.

On an official list of subscriptions we find the names of 107
localities in France, Algeria, Alsace-Lorraine, Germany, Italy,
Luxembourg, Sweden and Switzerland, totaling 65,678.75 francs.
Assistance from the Alliance was larger and with other Jewish
organizations, the amount received and distributed came to more
than 500,000 francs. Among the contributing groups were the *Hilfsverein der Deutschen Juden* in Berlin, the *Hilfsverein für die
osteuropäische Juden* at Frankfurt-am-Main, the Jewish Colonisation
Association in Paris, the *Israelitische Allianz* of Vienna, and various
American and English committees.

The Paris Alliance renewed a credit of 10,000 francs which it
had been giving for several years to school refectories. Also, it
continued to subsidize the loan funds set up in different places for
some time after the revolt. These were intended to help small shop
owners, craftsmen, and workers.

Still, the overall assistance of the Western Jewish organizations
was not sufficient and did not cover the material losses and the great
suffering of the victims. At this time, thousands of Jews sought
asylum in the large cities and even across the frontier in Austria,
Serbia and Bulgaria. Throughout the uprising 2,000 refugees were
supported by the population of Itcani and Suceava in Bukovina.

At the same time, using simple circulars, the government broadened its policy of expulsion from the countryside which had preceded the revolt.

There were several instances where the peasants opposed the expulsion of the Jews. In the commune of Dersca in the district of Dorohoi, when the mayor, Baron de Wesembeck, received the circular on evacuation, he convoked the villagers and asked their advice. They replied that the Jews were necessary for them and signed a request to the prefect asking for abrogation of the expulsion. The authorities paid no attention to the peasants' opposition and the Jews had to leave the village. In the district of Dorohoi there remained no trace of Jews in the countryside.

When the insurrection had been crushed, new circulars prohibited the Jews from returning to their former homes. To help the families hardest hit by the expulsions, the Vienna Alliance and other large Jewish organizations again distributed in 1908 the sum of 20,876 francs, most of it going to Bacau, Botosani, Jassy and Vaslui. The money distributed was ridiculously low and for many the only way out was the classical solution: emigration.

4. The Psychological Factor

To understand the depth of anti-Semitic feeling, one must turn to other disciplines such as psychoanalysis, the sociology of primitive man, anthropology. These new means of investigation furnish an answer to anti-Semitism as a permanent phenomenon of the Judeo-Christian civilization. But this lies outside the limits of our study.

However, let us content ourselves with recalling that the appearance of doctrinaire anti-Semitism and of organizations with extremist objectives as seen in their programs is closely bound to the convergence of the factors which we have already analyzed, but also to new manifestations of the psychological factor.

These manifestations have two dimensions, one is individual and personal, the other collective and social. On the individual level, we must stress that most of the Romanian anti-Semitic thinkers and agitators were deeply affected by myths, fantasies and traumas in the crystallization of their aversion towards the Jews. Anti-Semitism as a personal malady is the projection of a violently Manichean thought onto the symbol of evil, stereotyped as the "Jewish spectre."

In Romania, oppressive legislation and social discrimination aiming at complete isolation - even the Masonic lodges refused Jews - created and consolidated the image of the Jew as a social pariah. Characterizing the Romanian anti-Semites, Bernard Lazare wrote in his book *L'Antisémitisme, son histoire et ses causes*:

> They reproached the Jews for forming a state within the state, which was true, and, as a perpetual contradiction in anti-Judaism, they passed laws to maintain them in that condition, which they considered dangerous; they asserted that Jewish education deformed the brains of those who received it and that it made them unfit for social life, which was only too true, and finally they came to the point of forbidding the Jews from receiving the education given to Christians, which would have brought them out of their abasement.

Anti-Semitism as a social malady is the result of objective tensions, demographic expansion, the economic role, cultural and national identity and of emotional tensions produced by the collective subconscious.

The new psychological state of Romanian society was grafted onto classic anti-Judaism of religious origin and in this, hatred of the Jew "served as an outlet for the anxiety brought about by social disorder," as explained by Saul Friedlander in his book on Nazi anti-Semitism.

This disorder manifested itself especially in the cities which explains the relentlessness of the middle class against the Jews. It also explains why anti-Semitism had a "patriarchal" character in the countryside, where changes were much slower and where the majority of the people lived. This anti-Semitism had, nevertheless, a tenacious quality which made it very dangerous at times of crisis, as we have seen during the revolt of 1907.

5. Romanian Intellectuals Opposed to Anti-Semitism

We have had occasion to remark that, in opposition to the discriminatory attitude of the governments and their subaltern agents, a number of political personalities like Petre Carp, Titu

Maiorescu, Gheroghe Panu, and others, took a position in favor of
the emancipation of the Jews. However, their voices were too weak
to drown out the noise of an impatient and unbridled nationalist
movement.

In the last decade of the nineteenth century and the first of the
twentieth, with the penetration liberal thought, radical and socialist,
there arose a movement of public opinion, not very strong, it is true,
but which reacted courageously against the arbitrary government
policy towards the Jews, against the anti-Semitic organizations and
their actions.

In 1897, J.G. Miclescu, a section head in the Ministry of
Justice, a former deputy and an influential member of the Junimist
Society, published a series of articles on the Romanian Jews in the
review *Prutul* during the months of April, May and June. These
articles were collected in the same year in a brochure entitled *The
Jewish Question is a Moral Question*. Indignant at the cynical manner
in which the political parties exploited that question and moved by
the oppressive legislation, the author sounded a cry of alarm calling
for normalization of the situation of the Jews in Romania. After a
historical review of the anti-Jewish laws and regulations, he also
placed a brand of shame on the European anti-Semitic movement:

> After having given us a lesson in advanced civi-
> lization (in the Treaty of Berlin), it [Europe] is
> now offering us the comical spectacle of the anti-
> Semitism of Drumont in Paris, Stoeker in Berlin
> and Lueger in Vienna. We now have everywhere
> full freedom, both external and moral, to study
> the question and to examine with all necessary
> tranquillity whether what we have done was well
> done; if it was well done, we shall maintain the
> *status quo*, consciously and with full understand-
> ing; we shall change it if it was bad. As for me, I
> declare that things are going from bad to worse.
> For, although present legislation is possibly giving
> satisfaction to our national vanity, in exchange for
> this vain satisfaction, it is creating for us moral
> maladies which will destroy us from top to
> bottom.

Constantin Radulescu-Motru holds an important place in the struggle against anti-Semitism. He was a philosopher, psychologist, professor at the University of Bucharest and an incisive journalist. He managed the review *Noua Revista Romana* (The New Romanian Review) which appeared in two series from January 1, 1900 to January 15, 1902, and from October 12, 1908 to July 31, 1916. In the first year of its appearance, at the time of the Jewish emigration on foot, the review launched an inquiry on the Jewish question, soliciting the views of a number of personalities in various countries and publishing their replies. Except for two answers from Edouard Drumont and H.St. Chamberlain, which took a well-known reactionary position, all the others came out against racism and made strong pleas in favor of the emancipation of the Jews. Among them were Luigi Luzzati, Georges Clemenceau, Émile Zola, Anatole Leroy Beaulieu, Cesare Lombroso, Achile Loria, W.T. Stead, Ernest Moch, Charles Richet, and others. The shortest, but most significant reply came from Émile Zola:

Milan   August 7, 1900

Sir,
    Unfortunately I am not well acquainted with the political and social questions in Romania. But since you have asked me whether I should advise the Romanians to grant full equality in political and civic rights to the Jews, I answer without hesitation: Yes. I am in favor of the broadest equality and the greatest solidarity possible between all the people of the earth.

Cordially,
Émile Zola

Constantin Radulescu-Motru replied to the answer by H.St. Chamberlain in a resounding article. "It is useless," he declared, "for bands of Jews to wander from one end of the country to the other, looking for the crumbs that fall from the tables of the rich; it is useless for the whole world to mourn at seeing women and children suffering from hunger. The children of Israel are disguising themselves as beggars in order to rob us more easily!" In conclusion, the author said that in Romania the Jewish question is one of compensation:

> Foreign governments will be glad to allow us to have our Jews, with or without rights, in exchange for a compensation, a humiliation on our part. It was like that with the Germans after the question of independence and so it will be in the future with the stronger countries. Twenty years ago, Bismarck insisted on the buying back of the railroads as a price for not taking interest in the Jewish question under conditions which were advantageous for the German retirees; in the future, another Bismarck will ask us to vote for new tariffs in the interest of German trade. Everyone will ask us for something, and we shall be forced to give in because we insist on keeping our Semitic slaves instead of the gypsy ones we had before....

He supported giving citizenship to the Jews and was always a fighter on the side of anti-Semitism.

The journalist and democratic politician Constantin Mille courageously denounced discrimination against the Jews in the pages of *Adeverul* and other newspapers. He hailed the visit of Bernard Lazare in Romania in 1902 and his fight for his co-religionists.

In 1907, during the peasant revolt, a few Liberal publications reacted against the hatred propagated by Cuza and Iorga. The newspaper *Actiunea* wrote on May 20:

> We have allowed Mr. Cuza to propagate at the University of Jassy the most hideous illness of our time: xenophobia. We have allowed the famous Iorga to spread the most dangerous theories at Bucharest; under the banner of nationalism, we have allowed the youth to be excited...; we have allowed the most subversive ideas to be infused into the soul of our young people, the hatred of classes and of races, scorn for order and legality; finally, we have allowed this dangerous neuro-

pathy to expand in its incendiary review *Neamul Romanesc*, and we have seen its lucubrations produce their fruit as that journal was distributed free of charge in the countryside.

Ovid Desusianu (1873-1938), philologist, linguist and historian of Romanian literature, carried on a long fight against anti-Semitic agitation in his review *Viata noua* (New Life) from 1905 to 1925. In 1910, a group of young intellectuals of socialist orientation began to publish the review *Facla* (The Torch) under the direction of N.D. Cocea. That review cleverly attacked the opinions of Cuza and Iorga who had created the Nationalist Democratic Party in that same year. Among the contributors to that review were several who became famous in Romanian literature, such as the poet Tudor Arghezi and the novelist Gala Galaction, who translated the Bible into Romanian.

The dramatist Ion Luca Caragiale (1852-1912), the spiritual father of Eugene Ionescu, supported emancipation and painted Jewish portraits in his works with much understanding. This was also the case of Leiba Zibal in his novelette of 1889, *O faclie de pasti* (A Paschal Torch), and the great novelist Mihail Sadoveanu (1880-1961) in many of his works.

Although in general the Romanian socialists avoided taking a position on the Jewish problem, several, like Ion Nadejde (1854-1928) demanded from the beginning equality of civic and political rights for the Jews.

All of these attitudes and many others show us the existence of a current of public opinion favorable to integration of the Jews into the life of the country.

In opposition to this current the anti-Semitic nationalist movement counterattacked and in 1913 came the publication of three violent anti-Jewish pamphlets written by Bogdan Duica and N. Paulescu, both inspired by the book by Rohling, *The Talmud Jew*.

How did the Jews react, what palliative did they bring against the oppressive legislative policy and the rise of dangers symbolized by an anti-Semitic movement with broad bases among the people whose convulsions not only short-circuited attempts at finding social peace, as shown above, but increased through tensions which were always disquieting?

CHAPTER NINE

THE JEWISH REACTION: ASSIMILATION OR PARTICULARIZATION?

1. Socio-Economic Changes

At the end of the nineteenth century, the situation created for the Jews by a carefully graduated anti-Semitic legislation was the following: representatives of the middle class were excluded from all public employment, because the Jews could not be attorneys, physicians, exchange agents, brokers, employees in tobacco monopolies or state railways, or principals of schools. A number of commercial branches were also closed to them, such as that of druggist, liquor stores, groceries which sold tonic products, salesmen, farmers. Jewish workers were excluded from state-owned factories, the railways, public works and even private enterprises. Above all there floated the threat of expulsion without cause through the law on foreigners.

Nevertheless, or finally, we should recall that in spite of that ostracism, in spite of non-emancipation, the Jews continued after the Berlin Congress to play an important economic role. That role was recently described by Professor Nicholas Spulber in a comparative study on the place of the Jewish entrepreneur in Romania in the middle of the nineteenth century up to the Second World War and that of the Chinese businessmen in Indochina from the last quarter of the nineteenth century until the 1960s. Presenting the growth and decline of capital and the takers of risks in those two agrarian countries undergoing development, this was his conclusion:

> Without a doubt, the foreign entrepreneur sometimes uses cruel or illicit methods to acquire capital in the first phase of development; he compels the subsistence society which was so hermetically shut in onto itself to open towards the outside, changes it tastes, broadens its contact with the market, forcing it to diversify its activities and increases it dependence on trade, industry and the cities.

However, the social pyramid of the Jews underwent a transformation in the last twenty years of the nineteenth century and at the beginning of the twentieth in the following way: diminution in the number of businessmen, increase in the number of craftsmen and the emergence of a proletariat.

According to the industrial study by the Ministry of Public Land in 1901-1902, of a total of 107,332 licensed merchants, there were 22,590 Jews (21.1%); the number of craftsmen was 97,755 with 19,181 Jews (19.6%); of 625 industries 122 were Jewish (19.5%); and finally, of 39,121 workers and employees, 2,092 were Jews (5.3%).

The percentage Jews was much higher in Moldavia alone, where 75% of the Jewish population lived and where the merchants and workers constituted a majority in the large cities. On the basis of these data, which are not absolute, it has been concluded that about 90% of the Jewish population, or about 200,000, were living from trade and crafts in an almost equal proportion.

It may be noted that at the beginning of the twentieth century many of the craftsmen were recruited among foreigners. According to statistics from the Bucharest Chamber of Commerce in 1904, there were 18,644 craftsmen registered in the capital of whom 9,608 were Romanian citizens, 3,190 were Jews, 1,293 were Romanian subjects and the rest were Austro-Hungarians, Bulgars, Serbs, Greeks, Turks, Russians, Italians, Germans, Frenchmen and 24 of other nationalities.

In 1908 there were 127,840 craftsmen in Romania, with 83.1% in the cities and 16.69% in rural communes. From 1906 to 1910, according to the Ministry of the Treasury, the number of Romanian businessmen increased by 3,287 and the number of Jewish businessmen decreased by 1,665. The reduction in the number of Jewish businessmen was partly due to emigration, but most of the emigrants were craftsmen.

In spite of their large number, most of the craftsmen and merchants were of modest means; in case of economic crisis, generally caused by a bad harvest, they reached the limits of poverty. This was also due to the professional concentration of the Jews in light industry and building. This phenomenon, which was common in the countries of Eastern Europe, was explained by the Marxist sociologist Abraham Léon as the real cause of the large Jewish emigration at the end of nineteenth century. He wrote as follows:

> Whereas the blacksmith or the non-Jewish farmer
> found an outlet in the factories or mines, the
> Jewish masses which joined the proletariat entered
> small industries producing consumer goods. The
> process of transformation of the pre-capitalist
> Jewish merchant into a skilled worker met with
> another process, the elimination of the Jewish
> worker through machinery. This last influenced
> the former. The Jewish masses leaving the small
> towns were unable to join the proletariat and were
> compelled to emigrate.

This was their new social position conditioned by the economic forces which had a determining influence on the Jews and their reaction was not homogeneous.

Among the different tendencies and orientations, we can discern a bivalent dynamism: assimilation and particularization. Assimilation was recommended by the rich Jews, community leaders and those of the first generation of Jewish intellectuals. The former desired political and social assimilation while respecting the difference. Their struggle to obtain legal recognition of the communities, which was doomed to failure during the nineteenth century, and to obtain Jewish secular education illustrate this point of view. The latter desired more than assimilation - they looked for total integration into Romanian society. They sought to reach their own liberation and that of the Jewish working masses through socialism. An extremist minority tended towards obliteration of their Jewish roots, towards conversion.

Particularization existed on two levels: that of the Jewish groups oriented partly towards Orthodoxy and partly towards messianic Zionism.

2. The Socialist Ideal

Doctrinal socialism appeared in Romania with the writings of Constantin Dobogreanu Gherea (1855-1920) and those of other Russian political refugees. Socialism was propagated through study circles in the large cities of the country. A pleiad of militants grew around Gherea and the workers' movement underwent a change through the formation in 1893 of the Social Democratic Party of

Romanian Workers (P.S.D.M.R.). A series of publications spread socialist ideas during the last decade of the nineteenth century. The most important were *Munca* (1890-1894), *Lumea Noua* (The New World) published from 1894 to 1900, the first socialist daily in Romania, and *Democratia Sociala*.

One of the first Jewish defenders of socialist ideas was Dr. Stefan Stanca-Stein (1865-1897). In articles which he published in his review *Lumina*, collected into a book in 1892, he saw in the struggle of masses of Romanian and Jewish workers a guarantee for their future social and political liberation.

In May, 1895, several young Jews created in Jassy the socialist club *Lumina* which published from 19 April 1896 on, a Yiddish-language weekly called *Der Wecker* (The Alarm Clock) and once or twice a month the review *Lumina*, where the principles and theoretical orientation of the group were developed in the direction of international socialism and in liaison with the Social Democratic Party founded in 1893. They fought for the political emancipation of the Jews as a precondition for improvement in the condition of Jewish workers. The following excerpt from their analysis illustrates their socialist views:

> It is not our sole object to depict the situation of an impoverished people, but also to examine that situation from an economic point of view and to show the importance of the Jews in the material development of Romania. Political and economic activity is concentrated in the cities, which are the true centers of trade, industry and capital. In the cities Jews constitute the commercial and industrial element in a preponderant manner.

On the other hand, the Christian social strata were composed of the large landowners whom competition from outside Europe were about to ruin, of a depraved civil service and a motley bourgeoisie who were greatly inferior to the Jewish bourgeoisie with respect to professional quality. In Moldavia, that "Romanian" bourgeoisie was quite sparse and the city of Jassy only had forty real merchants.

Thus, the struggle of those classes against the Jewish population was at the same time a struggle of feudal and reactionary classes against the largest urban group. But to check the development of that element meant stopping the capitalist economy and at the same time stifling the proletariat in its beginnings. Thus, the iniquitous situation of the Jews in Romania, besides affecting the interests of the Jewish bourgeoisie, weighed heavily on the Jewish proletariat, making trade union, cultural and political organization of the Jewish workers impossible.

We have sketched the situation of the classes in Romania. On the one hand, we see the parallel development of the Jewish bourgeoisie and the proletariat, and on the other, the common interest of those two classes in obtaining political rights in Romania. As long as the Jewish proletariat - which, in Romania, was the proletariat par excellence - could not engage in political action, socialism could not create a powerful workers' party in Romania. The Jewish workers had to adopt the motto "the conquest of civic rights"; in that struggle the Jewish bourgeoisie quite naturally helped them. That special situation required special tactics on the part of the Socialist Party.

We have been reproached for taking the acquisition of political rights as the central theme of our demands; this would not favor the interests of the workers, but rather those of the bourgeoisie. It was necessary for the country's progress and for that of the proletariat. In Romania, the Jewish bourgeoisie was the most powerful agent of capitalism and it was the lack of political rights which prevented them from full expansion. The Jewish bourgeoisie had a reactionary side, but also a revolutionary one. Concerning it, one should take the position of Marx and Engels in 1847 to obtain rights enjoyed in common by the Prussian bourgeoisie and the Prussian proletariat.

That common ground between the Jewish bourgeoisie and the Jewish proletariat did not destroy the class difference between them and even though they fought together for equality of rights, they remained enemies from the economic point of view.

As for the Romanian socialists, their opinion was divided on the question of granting political rights to the Jews. Some feared that many Jewish voices would support the middle class parties and concluded that the Jews would have to wait for political freedom.

Others, among whom the socialist leader Ion Nadejde should be mentioned first of all, declared that the Jews ought to receive political rights. Ion Catina stated this point of view in the article "*Socialistii si Evreii*" (Socialists and Jews) in the review *Egalitatea* in 1891:

> The workers' party has the sacred duty of strug-
> gling for naturalization of the Jews who are called
> upon like Romanians to play a political role. The
> strongest argument opposing this struggle is that
> political rights will be given to the Jewish
> bourgeoisie as well. Certainly, but we shall have
> 70 Jewish citizens who are workers and only 30,
> or fewer, who are bourgeois citizens.

The same Ion Catina organized an appeal signed by 400 Romanian citizens calling for emancipation of the Jews.

The Social Democratic Party underwent a serious schism in 1899 causing its temporary dissolution and a number of dissidents publicly expressed their anti-Semitic feelings. The activity of the socialists in general and the Jewish socialists in particular worried the authorities and the government used the law on foreigners against them. Several were banished, including Adolphe Clarnet, who went to France, where he published in 1903 a brochure entitled *The Romanian Jews.*

When the Social Democratic Party was reformed in 1910, a growing number of Jews joined it.

The second series of *Der Wecker,* the organ of the Jewish socialist group in Jassy, was at the same time a local publication of the Social Democratic Party. As a socialist newspaper, *Der Wecker* aimed at explaining the main socio-political events of the time and at militating for development of the class consciousness of the exploited Jewish population. One read on August 29, 1915, in an article devoted to the forming of trade unions:

> Jewish worker, you who are being exploited as
> much by your Jewish manager as by the
> Romanian oligarchy, joined the union so that,
> together with your Romanian working brothers,
> you can improve your situation and obtain the
> greatest number of human rights. They have been
> trampling on you for too long!

The theme of the publication, anchored in the realities of the period, reflected the problems which concerned the masses of Jewish workers. *Der Wecker* militated for gaining democratic freedom and political rights. It drew the attention of the workers to the fact that, in their struggle for citizens' rights, they must not count on the Jewish bourgeoisie, for the latter was using all means to gain the goodwill of the governing classes, thus forming with them a front against those who were being exploited. The newspaper often reminded its readers that the only party which had fought for the granting of political rights to the Jews was the Social Democratic Party. Article 10 of the socialist program read as follows: "Full rights for native Jews, i.e., civic and political rights, equal to Romanian citizens." At all the conventions, in the press, at many popular meetings, the Jewish problem was discussed. But Article 10 was only accepted after a stormy debate, for many socialists were opposed to it.

Expressing the concept of the Social Democratic Party, *Der Wecker* saw the solution to the situation of the proletariat, and of the Jewish worker in particular, through the creation of a new society without the exploitation of one person by another. Demanding equality of civic and political rights, the editors opposed Jewish nationalism, as they opposed Romanian or any other.

Encouraging the development of Yiddish, the language of the Jewish workers, and a popular Jewish culture, the socialist group in Jassy was close to the ideas of the *Algemeyner Yidisher Arbeter Bund*, founded by the Jewish Socialist Party in Russia in 1897, concerning cultural autonomy.

However, as it only advanced socialist ideals and avoided Jewish nationalism, *Der Wecker* did not attract a large number of readers and soon disappeared. Although they were a minority, the Jewish socialist intellectuals who gravitated around this review left their mark both on the Jewish man in the street as well as on the Romanian socialist movement.

3. The Zionist Revolution

"As far as national consciousness is concerned," wrote Professor Jacob Katz in volume XI for UNESCO, "on the threshold of modern times, the Jews were better prepared to form a national movement than any other ethnic group in Europe." This was particularly true for the Jews of eastern Europe and in our case, for Romania. The barriers erected by xenophobic legislation had increased the isolation of the Jews. Speaking Yiddish, living in

communities closed in upon themselves, undergoing periodic persecution, it is not surprising that the hope of redemption, which, in
Jewish thinking, was always associated with the national destiny,
should find among the Romanian Jews fertile ground for its growth.

It was the journalist Armand Lévy who popularized in the
pages of the newspapers *Espérance* and *L'Israélite roumain* the idea
of the agricultural development of Eretz Israel. We have found a
letter from a Jewish physician from Giurgiu sent to the president of
the Jewish Alliance at Paris on May 29, 1867, which shows that as
early as then there were many Jews who cherished the Zionist ideal.
Learning from *Espérance* of the plan to establish a Jewish colony in
Palestine, Dr. Wertheimer asked: "Is it the purpose of this colonization to prepare the way for our nation and the restoration of Israel,
or is it simply to make farmers of the Jews and thus make their daily
life easier?"

The answer was that "the idea of the Alliance was not at all to
encourage emigration to Jerusalem, but to help the Jews of Palestine
by encouraging agriculture." This answer indicated the attitude of
the Alliance and it seems, at least at that time, that "the only purpose
of the Jewish Alliance was emancipation by assimilation," as Iouda
Tchernoff wrote in Paris in 1937.

Rabbi S. Taubes, a leading figure in Romanian Judaism, and
Armand Lévy had a meeting in 1868 with Minister Bratianu on the
subject of the Jews in Romania. The latter explained to them that his
policy towards the Jews was conditioned by their large number and
declared that at least ten thousand families should leave the country
at once. He even promised them to obtain money from the Romanian
parliament to encourage emigration. The two Jewish leaders
supported the project which they hoped would take the form of Eretz
Israel, but in spite of their efforts, it did not come to pass.

The thought of colonizing Eretz Israel by the Jews of Romania
came up again during discussion of the proposal of Consul Peixotto
concerning emigration from the country in 1872, but was rejected in
favor of continuing the struggle for political emancipation.

Zvi Kalischer (1795-1874) a German rabbi of Polish origin,
who witnessed as a youth the emancipation of the Jews in France and
the German countries at the time of Napoleon, occupies an important
place in the Jewish national movement prior to Herzl. He reached the
conclusion that the political emancipation already obtained by the
Western Jews was only a stage necessary towards assembling at least

part of the Jewish people in Palestine. He wrote that the situation of the Jews in Romania was "an evil from which good would come." In a letter to the editor of the newspaper *Ha-Zofe be-Eretz ha-hadasha*, he stated that even if "a small number of Romanian Jews formed colonies in Palestine, that would have favorable repercussions on the situation of their brothers, for the Romanians would be convinced that the Jews were useful and necessary for them."

The idea of agricultural colonization in Eretz Israel spread quickly among the Romanian Jews and in 1875 a society called *Ishub Eretz Israel* (The Colonization of Eretz Israel) was founded at Moinesti. Similar societies were created in other cities under the leadership of the dynamic Eleazar Rokeach and a turning point was reached in the new movement of Jewish national renaissance at the Focsani conference of 30 December 1881 and 1 January 1882. Fifty-six delegates representing 29 localities took part in that conference which was held symbolically in the city where the union of the two principalities had been proclaimed. It was decided to encourage and coordinate all efforts towards organized emigration and successful colonization in Palestine. The conference had great impact on the Jews and one immediate result was the departure of the ship *Thetis* from Galatz in August, 1882, bearing 228 immigrants and the creation of the first farming colonies, Samarin-Zichron and Roch Pina. A new era had begun in the modern history of the Jews. Other organizations followed *Ishub Eretz Israel*, of which the largest was *Hovévé Zion* (The Lovers of Zion) in 1892.

The great figures in the beginnings of Zionism in Romania, Dr. Karpel Lippe (1830-1915) and Samuel Pineles (1843-1928), took up the cause of Theodore Herzl and at the Zionist congress at Basel in 1897, the former opened the debate as senior in age and the latter was appointed co-vice president. A contemporary publication noted that "The Romanian Zionists have done everything in their power to insure the success of the Congress by sending 25 kilos of petitions signed by nearly 50,000 Jews who requested transfer to the Holy Land" (*Der Baseler Kongress*, Vienna, 1897).

From 1897 to 1905, the Zionist program was propagated in Jewish publications and press in Yiddish, Hebrew, and Romanian, including the conclusion of the first congress which proposed the establishment of a Jewish state.

Sionistul became the official organ of the Zionist Federation in Romania which, following the death of Theodore Herzl in 1904, continued his efforts according to the decisions of the various Zionist conventions.

As early as 1898, at the fourth congress of *Hovévé Zion*, which was held at Galatz from 5 to 6 April 1898, it was unanimously decided to join in Herzl's cause, accepting the Basel platform. That brought new expansion to the Zionist movement and by 1899 there were 136 Zionist associations in Romania. Intellectuals soon joined the small businessmen and the working classes which formed the initial basis of the Zionist movement. But Herzl's death and internal dissensions weakened the movement. In 1905, the dynamic Heinrich Rosenbaum, who had played an important part together with Herzl in the creation of the Colonial Bank and the publication of the unofficial weekly *Die Welt*, became president of the Zionist Federation of Romania. He threw himself fully into the Zionist struggle, intensifying its propaganda and increasing its sections, but by 1907 he suddenly withdrew from Jewish political life. Later it was learned that he had undergone conversion to Roman Catholicism. In 1915 he wrote that a Jew converted to Christianity could remain a good Jew and a good Zionist.

Despite the repercussions of the peasant revolt, the Zionists of Romania took part in the eighth Zionist congress at The Hague. Their delegation included Dr. H. Moscovici, H. Schein, S. Pineles and the rabbis Dr. I. Nacht and Dr. I. Niemirower. We learn from the report by Rabbi Dr. I. Nacht, that the principal activity of the Romanian Zionist associations included, besides encouragement of emigration to Israel, two main points: Jewish education and fund raising.

By 1907, there were many independent Zionist societies in Romania and Zionist groups existed in nearly all the Jewish communities.

While supporting the idea of a return to Eretz Israel, the Romanian Zionists fought steadily for political emancipation.

Thus the Zionist movement experienced growth, but because of opposition by Turkish authorities, the number of Jews who established themselves in Palestine was small, although it still amounted to several thousand. The Balfour Declaration on November 2, 1917, found a resounding echo in Romania and represented there, as elsewhere, a turning-point in the Zionist movement.

"After twenty centuries of sleep and useless agitation, the Jewish people has begun to understand little by little that the only solution to the Jewish question is its recognition as a nation, as a people among others." This statement appeared in April, 1898, in the newspaper *Ahavat Zion*, and indicates the real revolution which had taken place in Jewish consciousness in Romania, where Jews were "foreigners not subject to foreign protection": this was the Zionist revolution.

4. Emigration

The activities of anti-Semitic organizations and particularly the serious economic crisis which struck Romania in 1899-1900 had fateful consequences for the entire Jewish population, but especially for the small merchants and craftsmen, and a trend towards emigration which had begun in 1899 soon acquired the speed of an exodus. The picture sketched by L. Descos, First Secretary at the Legation of France in Bucharest, in a report to his superior, reveals many aspects of the situation of the Romanian Jews. He wrote, in part:

> Considered foreigners, although subject to the obligations of Romanian citizens, deprived of political rights, unable to live in the countryside or to purchase rural property, threatened at any moment with expulsion by administrative order, they are living a difficult and disreputable life.... The crisis has caused inevitable havoc in this impoverished community of 269,000 Jews. Without buyers, without credit, the small tradesmen have gone bankrupt, the artisans have had no work; and their excessive misery has resulted in the last few months in a current of emigration which is only increasing. Interviewed on this by journalists, the principal leaders of the Jewish community have expressed their feelings about this emigration: the rabbis seem to look upon it with regret and the bankers with pleasure. While going back to the well-known crisis, they saw in it also a result of the new laws on licenses and traveling salesmen. Besides, they attribute to it a

renewed outbreak of anti-Semitism as well as the development of Zionism. In fact, there is a central Zionist committee at Galatz, affiliated with the Zionist organization of Vienna, which controls all the societies in Romania; Bucharest alone has seven of them. The royal government seems to be annoyed by the present Jewish emigration: it is afraid it will lead to a weakening in the economy and may be grounds for bringing Romania into discredit; therefore, they are trying to check it as far as possible. They are making it more difficult to obtain a passport and have even expelled a Jewish student named Juresco who was chairman of an emigration committee in Bucharest. Besides, this emigration is giving rise to very strange phenomena: in almost every city where there are Jews, that is in Moldavia and eastern Wallachia, the emigrants are forming small groups, taking an oath of solidarity to each other at the synagogue and are then leaving *on foot*, earning a little money as they go by giving shows or by publishing a single issue of a newspaper....

The emigration of the Romanian Jews on foot was the most unusual and most dramatic aspect of the great Jewish emigrations in Eastern Europe at the end of the nineteenth century and the beginning of the twentieth.

As they walked, certain groups sang in Romanian or in Yiddish. They were poor and suffered from hunger and in many towns free kitchens were created to feed them, subsidized by the Universal Jewish Alliance. Between May, 1900, and January, 1901, it spent about 500,000 francs to aid the impoverished. In the beginning, the various Western Jewish organizations opposed the very idea of emigration, but they ended by accepting it as a necessity.

On June 27 and 28, 1900, there was a meeting at Paris which produced the following resolutions:

1. Mass emigration such as that which occurred in May and June constitutes a danger which must be fought and stopped; emigration should continue,

but after having been organized and regulated by
strict rules.
2. Urgent distributions of aid must be made in
Romania to preserve the Jews of that country
from despair and famine.
3. The non-execution by Romania of Article 44 of
the Berlin Treaty constitutes a permanent violation of that diplomatic document; this side of the
Jewish question in Romania must not be over-
looked.

Far from slowing down, the emigration movement which was
partly supported by the Jewish Colonization Association only
increased. Bands of miserable Jews appeared at the railway stations
and ports of neighboring countries on their way to America. In view
of the expansion of emigration, the governments of the neighboring
countries, and particularly the Austro-Hungarian authorities,
informed the Romanians that they would not allow any emigrants to
cross their borders unless they possessed railway tickets for a
country other than theirs. Then the Romanian government changed
its attitude and attempted to slow down emigration by not issuing
passports except to groups of Jews bound for the United States,
Canada or Argentina with sufficient resources to reach at least
Hamburg, London and Paris.

Following the publication of the law concerning the different
trades, Jewish emigration increased in 1902. The Association of
Jewish Artisans published a manifesto calling for mass emigration.
According to statistics from the Jewish Alliance based on the number
of passports issued, 41,754 Jewish, men, women, and children left
Romania between 1899 and 1904. Among them were 9,288 artisans.
According to a report by the British Consul General at Galatz,
Colonel Trotter, dated January 28, 1903, between 1900 and 1902,
most of the emigrants went to New York, and somewhat fewer to
Philadelphia, London, Paris and the smallest number to Egypt and
Argentina.

As most of the emigrants went to the United States, the
American government circulated the Hay Note to the signatory
powers of the Berlin Treaty. It proposed that these powers seek an
effective means to insure respect for Article 44 of the Treaty. The
British government was favorable to the contents of that note and

sent a circular to the other signatory powers asking for joint measures to be taken to aid the Romanian Jews.

In Romania itself, to which the Note had not been sent officially, there was a loud reaction to it and the principal newspapers protested, denying the United States the right to intervene in that country's internal affairs. However, in spite of efforts made by France and England, there was no sequel to the American Note and the Romanian Jews were left to their fate.

Bernard Lazare made himself the symbol of revolt and indignation against the silence which surrounded the Jewish question in Romania. He wrote in February, 1902: "To ask Europe today, which, in violation of the Berlin Treaty, permitted the massacre of thousands of Christian Armenians by Muslims...to prevent a Christian people from making a hundred thousand Jews die of poverty and starvation would be too great an irony...."

His anger was directed likewise against rich Jews and, having introduced the phrase "Jewish nationalism," expressed his resentment in this way on August 9, 1900, in the magazine *L'Aurore*:

> One must give the Christian world justice that the solidarity of the Jewish world is not moved much more. In all the countries of Europe, the rich Jews - that mud of Israel - threw their contribution to the ragged emigrants at their doorstep, then they turned their heads away. They have given very little, in secrecy, in order not to be compromised by those unfortunate brothers who remind them of a past which makes them blush, they who are Frenchmen of France, Germans of Germany, who would have invented with the enthusiasm of neophytes any nationalism except a Jewish one.

In order to see for himself the real situation of the Jewish communities, this illustrious defender of Captain Dreyfus, whom Charles Péguy later referred to as "an atheist streaming with the word of God" in a book about himself and his friend entitled *Notre Jeunesse* (1910), made a trip to Galicia and Romania. He only visited Jassy and Bucharest, where he was warmly received by Jewish leaders and Zionists. After violent anti-Semitic demonstrations in opposition to his visit and because it had led to new hope among Romanian Jews, especially the proletariat, he was forced to depart precipitously. After his trip he wrote for *"L'Aurore* on June 21, 1902:

> ...One knows what is taking place in the Romania of the speculator-king Carol. The police can arrest fleeing Jews on the highways, can force them to return home without bread, a home which may have no roof; they can put the leaders of the emigration in prison and terrorize the Jewish quarters of Bucharest as they did after my departure, placing camps of gendarmes in the courtyards of synagogues and prohibiting shows in the Jewish theaters. But it cannot prevent the truth from being known. If even the financiers, Jewish or not,...want to establish momentarily Romanian credit, that country must stop treating 260,000 people who pay taxes from which the Romanian nationals live and who do their military service as serfs. If public opinion in Europe is unable to obtain that result, I hope that the Jewish proletariat in Romania will be able to obtain it for itself. To do so, it must be organized in a revolutionary manner and, together with the oppressed peasantry, its brothers in suffering, together with the Christian proletariat, it can conquer for them and for itself its rights and freedom.

The revolutionary solution suggestion by B. Lazare did not take place and while emigration continued - up to the Great War, nearly one-third of the Jewish community (about 90,000 persons) left the country - there was no change in the legal situation of the Jews.

CHAPTER TEN

WAR AND EMANCIPATION
OF THE JEWS

1. The 1913 Campaign

In 1912, Bulgaria, Serbia, Greece, and Montenegro attacked Turkey to rescue their Christian nationals who were still under Ottoman control. After the victory, the conquered territories had to be divided up and serious dissension broke out among the conquerors. Facing demands by Bulgaria, the former allies requested help from Romania, which hastened to agree. The Romanian army crossed the Danube on July 1, 1913, and quickly advanced on Sofia. Part of the troops occupied southern Dobrudja, which was the real objective of the campaign. There were no battles with the Bulgarian army. Considering any opposition useless, Bulgaria was forced to ask for peace, which was concluded at Bucharest on July 28 or August 10, 1913. Romania gained this region, known as the Quadrilateral, which was divided into two districts, Durastor and Caliacra.

What was the attitude of the Jews towards these events and what were the repercussions of the campaign on their legal status?

In 1910, in order to facilitate their fight to obtain political rights, several associations united and created the Union of Native Jews (*Uniunea Evreilor Pamanteni*), which was to become later on the only political organization representing Romanian Judaism. It grew quickly and whereas it only had two sections at the end of its first year, there were 51 by 1912; 80 by 1914; and 87 by 1916, with 12,000 members.

The first Union action was to send a petition to the Chamber of Deputies, asking it to examine the Jewish question "in a spirit of impartiality and justice." This petition, couched in moving and patriotic phrases, had no result and some voices were heard within the Jewish community saying that initiatives of that kind were useless and would never achieve anything. In their view, the solution to the question of emancipation lay solely in the pressure of the Great Powers.

During the Balkan War, the Western Jewish organizations redoubled their efforts to draw the attention of their respective governments to the situation of the Jews in Romania, hoping to attain their emancipation in the framework of an overall arrangement in the Balkans.

The American Immigration and Distribution League sent a letter to the French Minister of Agriculture, M. Pams, on July 12, 1912. In England, the Conjoint Jewish Committee, composed of the Jewish Board of Deputies and the Anglo-Jewish Association, sent a letter signed by their respective presidents, David Alexander and Claude Montefiore, asking Sir Edward Grey to refuse support of Romania if it continued to refuse to apply Article 44 of the Berlin Treaty.

Angelo Sereni, president of the Committee of Jewish Communities, asked many influential officials of his country to intervene and on March 3, 1913, Luigi Luzzati, a former prime minister, called the Jewish question to the attention of the public by a powerful article published by the *Corriere della Sera*, which ended on this prophetic note:

> By spontaneously emancipating the Jews, it (i.e., Romania) would at the same time free its soul of those sins which cannot be expiated, as they have their roots in persecution and intolerance. If it does not spontaneously emancipate them, *it will later be compelled to do it*, not only by the Great Powers, but also by the incoercible and inviolable power of human dignity and human freedom.

During full mobilization, the sectors which were most hostile were surprised to see the eagerness of the Jews to fulfill their military obligation. There were about 25,000 Jews who answered the call, including thousands of volunteers in addition to those subject to military service under the law. Jewish hospitals, schools and even synagogues were placed at the disposition of the authorities. Jews participated generously in the collection made to help the widows and orphans of those who were mobilized, contributing half of the total of four million francs, according to estimates made at that time. Many leaders expressed their satisfaction with this surge of patriotism.

In a session of the Senate on July 4, 1913, Emile Lahovary stressed that the Jews had answered the call "with the same enthusiasm as Romanian citizens." "Without violating constitutional norms," he said, "we shall surely find a way to hasten the naturalization of all those who have been mobilized."

Ovid Densusianu declared that giving naturalization to Jews who took part in the mobilization "would not only be an act of generosity, but a duty." And Take Ionescu said:

> The Jews have conducted themselves very well. Consequently, everywhere and without any prior agreement, the word has gone out that we should naturalize the Jews who were mobilized. Now it is certain that this will be done. If, on this occasion, the very equitable principle is also accepted that when an individual is naturalized immediately, this measure will have a greater impact than could have been hoped for.

A large movement took place, involving also the newspapers of widely different kinds, to hasten the solution of emancipation.

There was a divergence of opinion as to how it could be done and generally the individual method was preferred, but at least one thing seemed to have been gained, as we have seen: the naturalization as a group of those who had been under arms.

The question of equal rights for the Jews was not brought up at the peace conference in Bucharest and once the period of diplomatic successes had passed, the historical political parties and the Anti-Semitic organizations resumed their agitation.

Although various Western Jewish organizations continued their representations like those of the American Romanian Emancipation Committee to the French government, new decrees were issued concerning the Jews. For example, at the beginning of 1914, the famous law for controlling foreigners was passed, giving the Minister of the Interior the right to force the "foreigner" to leave the area where he lived and go to a specially-selected place. Lower-ranking officials often abused this law when applying it to Jews.

At this point, the Union of Native Jews did not give up and continued its struggle to improve the situation of the Jews and to obtain equal rights. Through its publication *Infratirea*, it rallied wider and wider sections of the Jewish population.

2. World War I and the Jews

King Carol died on October 10, 1914, without heir and by virtue of a special law of 1889 his nephew Ferdinand was named as his successor. When he ascended the throne, Europe was at war. In spite of the secret treaty of 1883 which aligned Romania with the Central Powers, it remained neutral for two years.

Finally, in order to complete its status as a national state and after having signed a secret treaty with the countries of the Triple Alliance on August 17 which gave it Transylvania, Bukovina and the Banat, Romania declared war on Austria-Hungary on August 27, 1916.

The declaration of war surprised the Central Powers which did not expect it until later, after the harvest at the end of September. Because of his error in judgment, Falkenhayn was relieved and sent to the new front in Transylvania with five divisions of infantry and one of cavalry which had been transferred from the eastern and western fronts.

After their first successes in Transylvania against the Austro-Hungarian army, which were relatively easy, the Romanian forces had to retreat when facing the Germans. When they were also attacked from the south in Dobrudja, the Romanian armies, which were insufficiently equipped, had to withdraw and the capital was occupied. The front was stabilized south of Moldavia on the Siret line.

After a hard winter, and with the help of the French military mission under General Berthelot and with ammunition received from the West, the Romanian army was regrouped and on July 24, 1917, succeeded in breaking through in the area of Marasti. A second offensive was to have taken place on the Siret (River) but, under the influence of the Revolution, the Russian troops did not appear and the Romanian attack had to be stopped. Mackenson, commanding the German forces, launched a major offensive aimed at occupying the whole the Moldavia, but in spite of the superiority of his troops in number and technique, he was unable to break the front. The Romanian soldiers fought brilliantly in the battles of Marasti and Marasesti.

The Bolshevik Revolution and the peace of Brest-Litovsk, which opened the Ukraine to the German and Austro-Hungarian armies, compelled the Romanian government, which had moved to

Jassy and whose country was not occupied but was now encircled, to ask for peace.

The treaty of May 7, 1918, which was never ratified, imposed very heavy economic and territorial conditions on the country: all industry, trade and finance were subjected to German oversight. Dobrudja was recovered and also a section of the frontier in the Carpathian mountains which included 170,000 Romanian villagers.

The Bucharest Treaty, which also contained a clause concerning the equalization of religious belief to which we shall return later, could not take effect in time, because the development of the war in Europe precipitated an outcome favorable to the Allies and Germany had to ask for peace on November 11, 1918.

Mobilized again on November 10, the Romanian army crossed the Carpathians where the Transylvanian Romanians greeted them with joy: a chapter of history was ended.

By the treaty of Saint-Germain-en-Laye, which it signed on December 9, 1919, Romania became larger and reached completion of its national borders. At the same time it agreed to recognize its Jewish subjects as citizens with full rights. How did this result come about?

From the beginning of hostilities, about 25,000 Jews were serving in the Romanian army. Just as in the War for Independence in 1877 and in the campaign of 1913, the Jews again were solidly behind the fight for their country. Many Jewish girls and women left their families to devote themselves to the sick and wounded. Even the poorest Jewish communities made large sacrifices and large sums of money were given to the Red Cross. All Jewish institutions gave their space and liquid money for public service.

On the same day as that of the declaration of war, the Union of Native Jews published this important manifesto:

> As in 1877 and in 1913, native Jews, taking into account above all the higher needs of the country which asks, in the interest of union, to set aside discontent and renounce as long as the war lasts all particular political claims, will from today on place all their spiritual and material energy as well as their strength at the disposition of the country, in order to attain most rapidly the only objective we should have today: victory.

Despite these manifestations of active patriotism, the Jews still had to suffer many exactions during the war coming from civil and military authorities.

A few months before the start of the war, hundreds of Jewish families were expelled from towns on the frontier and the application of the law against espionage as applied to innocent Jewish residents often had the character of a systematic campaign.

There are many reports which unanimously attest the active Anti-Semitism existing in the army and especially among the officers.

Still, the Jews fought valiantly and after the war many statistics pointed to their active participation. At war's end, the Jews had the right to expect a radical change in their condition and recognition of their full citizenship.

3. Emancipation of the Jews

The Bucharest Peace Treaty was an important marker on the long road which finally led to recognition of equal civic and political rights for the Jews. To be sure, that treaty was never ratified and its stipulations were annulled by the later turn of events, but it still was an important date in the political evolution of the Jewish problem in Romania.

In fact, Articles 27 and 28 of Chapter V deal with the "Equalization of Religious Organizations in Romania".

Article 27 proclaims the equality of minority cults in Romania with the Orthodox cult. Article 28 concerns the Jews directly:

> A difference in religious belief cannot exert in Romania any influence on civil status and in particular on political and civil rights. The principle expressed above will take effect also with respect to the nationalization of Romanian residents who are not under foreign protection, including the Jews who have been considered up to now as foreigners. To this end, it will be decreed in Romania, until ratification of the peace treaty, that in all cases, those who are not subject to other laws and who have taken part in the war, either in the armed services or in the auxiliary

services, or who were born in the country and
have their domicile in it, will be classed, without
other consideration, among Romanian citizens,
enjoying all rights, and may be registered as such
in the Tribunal. The acquisition of Romanian citizenship will likewise extend to legitimate spouses,
to widows and to the minor children of such
persons.

What was new in this article resides in the fact that means for
application of civil and political equality were offered. The system of
naturalization *en bloc* replaced individual naturalization; a <u>right</u> to
naturalization was substituted for special naturalizations, and finally,
the judicial institution which made a final judgment on naturalization
henceforth had only the simple role of recording it.

As a result of this treaty, the Romanian government, headed
by M. Marghiloman, promulgated on August 27, 1918, the law
concerning naturalization of foreigners born in the country.

The first article provided that "foreigners in Romania who are
not subjects of another State, without distinction of religion, are
declared Romanian citizens if they fulfill the conditions necessary to
belong to the following categories...." Under the nine paragraphs of
that article, the four following categories of native Jews were
naturalized:

(1) Those who served in the army, in whatever
position, during the war;
(2) Those born in Romania of parents also born in
Romania;
(3) Those who took part in the Bulgarian campaign in 1913;
(4) The spouses and children of all those falling
into these categories.

Due to the evolution of the war and the German disaster, the
Marghiloman government fell and the new Prime Minister, Ion I.
Bratianu, the son of Ion Bratianu, annulled the decisions of his
predecessor.

Knowing the position of the Allies on the question and that
they had decided to have the rights of the Jews recognized, the

government of Ion I. Bratianu took the initiative and on December 20, 1918, published a new decree-law bearing the number 3902.

Under that decree, the following categories of Jews were naturalized:

> (1) Those who had taken part in the campaign of 1913 or the World War;
> (2) Those born in the country and who are not under the protection of a foreign power;
> (3) The spouses, legitimate children, even minors and widows of the preceding categories and those who had gone through the system of individual naturalization.

The new decree-law differed very little from the preceding one, but was wider in that it allowed naturalization of persons born in the country without requiring them to prove the birth of their parents.

The application of that decree, like that of the earlier one, met with a major difficulty in that the requester, even though he had all the necessary papers, still had to go through a full hearing, the only difference being that now it was not the Parliament but the courts which granted naturalization.

The Union of Native Jews opposed the new decree, saying that "it was not a social law which could help the mass of the Jewish population, but only a few privileged persons who had the time and money." It asked for a law of emancipation for all Jews without any other form of procedure than that of a simple publication.

On February 21, 1919, the president of the Jewish Alliance in Paris sent a letter on the same subject to the French Minister of Foreign Affairs, listing the grievances against the Bucharest decree-law as follows:

> We regret to note that the decree-law does not greatly change the legal situation of the Romanian Jews since:
> (a) it only authorizes individual naturalizations;
> (b) it subjects the right of citizenship to the arbitrary decision of a magistrate;

(c) it requires the postulant to furnish proof,
which is almost impossible, that he was
never the subject of a foreign country.

In view of the continuation of the restrictive policy of the Romanian government, the president of the Jewish Alliance believed that action by the Allied and Associated Powers was necessary to regulate this question in a definitive manner and without ambiguity, as it had held the attention of the chanceries for half a century.

"We believe we can hope," he concluded, "that the delegates of the (French) Republic, continuing the traditions of French diplomacy, will take up the just cause of the Romanian Jews as they did at the Berlin Congress."

The Jewish Alliance also turned to the delegates of the Great Powers to the peace conference and the Commission on New States, sending them a memorandum on the Jewish question on March 21, 1919.

All of these efforts were not in vain and the Jewish organizations received assurance that the final treaty would take into consideration the case of the Romanian Jews.

Under pressure from the discussions which had taken place at the peace conference in Paris, the Romanian government promulgated a new decree-law on May 22, 1919, which was much more liberal in tone than the preceding one. In it, the decision of the courts on naturalization was replaced by a simple statement by the postulant. However, it was issued during the absence of the parliament, which, as in the case of the earlier decrees, made it provisional.

Meanwhile, at the peace conference, the problem of the Romanian Jews was solved in the framework of the Peace Treaty of Saint-Germain-en-Laye. Because of its clauses on the status of minorities which brought about the successive resignations of the governments of I.C. Bratianu and General A. Vaitoianu, it was not signed by Romania until December 9, under Prime Minister Coanda.

That treaty proclaimed complete freedom of religion and the civil and political emancipation of all Romanian Jews.

In the manner of their formulation, the articles of the Treaty read like parts of a constitution. Articles 1, 7 and 8 gave definite sanction to emancipation:

Article 1: Romania agrees that the stipulations
contained in Articles 2 and 8 of the present
chapter be recognized as basic laws, that no law,
regulation or any official act may be in contradiction or opposition to them and that no law,
regulation or any official act may prevail against
them.

Article 7: Romania agrees to recognize as
citizens, with full rights and without any formality, Jews living in all its territory and who cannot
take advantage of any other nationality.

Article 8: All Romanian citizens will be equal
before the law and enjoy the same civil and political rights without distinction of race, language, or
religion.

A difference in religion, belief or faith will
not hinder any Romanian citizen in the enjoyment
of civil and political rights, especially for admission to public office, functions and honors or the
exercise of different professions or industries.

No restriction will be placed on the free use by
any Romanian citizen of any language whatsoever
in private or commercial relations, whether in
matters of religion, press or publications of any
kind, or in public meetings.

Notwithstanding the establishment by the
Romanian government of an official language,
reasonable facilities will be given Romanian
citizens speaking a language other than Romanian
to use their language either orally or in writing in
the courts.

Merit for the equitable solution to emancipation of the Jews in
Romania as incorporated in the peace treaty belongs to French
diplomacy first of all. The provisions of that treaty received legislative sanction through modification of the constitution in 1923 which
replaced Article 7 by Article 133, granting civil and political rights
to all the Jews of Greater Romania.

CONCLUSION

History is mutilated perception, according to G.R. Elton in his book *The Practice of History*, published by the Sydney University Press in 1969. This is particularly true in a study of social relations and mental attitudes expressed through the medium of languages and representations undergoing change. Any judgment of value is based on a nominalist conception of history, because the past is being constantly enriched and receives a retroactive sense of the future. This increases the difficulty of the scholar and the ideal approach will never be more than asymptotic.

It is not an easy thing to grasp the outstanding traits of Judeo-Christian relations in modern times and in the framework of a society undergoing drastic change. To present these relationships in the perspective of constant tension naturally creates a certain distortion of the general historical picture. That is why, when we took up the task of understanding a universal phenomenon of Christian civilization in a county which came late to join the concert of European nations, we thought it necessary to go far back into its history. We learned of the tenacity with which the Romanian people were able to endure and maintain their personality in an extremely hostile environment.

The fate of the Jews in the Romanian lands up to 1866 was not that caused by a single series of persecutions and lamentations. It was not the unfavorable daily relationships which conditioned the situation of the Jews: for a long time their status depended on the authority of the prince. In spite of a number of exclusions, it was not a question of intolerance and the various waves of Jewish immigration, which were encouraged in most cases, were well received in the Romanian lands. Playing the role of a middle-class in a society which was essentially agrarian, from the end of the eighteenth and up to the middle of the nineteenth century, the Jews contributed to the urbanization of Moldavia. The growing position of the Jews in trade and crafts was accompanied after 1848 by the awakening of Romanian nationalism and a study in social psychology is not needed to state that these two concomitant phenomena created a climate favorable to the blossoming of a Jewish problem.

That problem appeared in its most acute legal form at the time of the Organic Laws. The Jews suffered from the use of Tsarist methods which excluded them from many things which had not been known before: they were considered foreigners and, as non-

Christians, were not allowed to regain their lost rights through naturalization. This differentiation was made official in 1866 by Article 7 of the Constitution, marking a reversal of the liberal measures issued by Prince Cuza, who had unified Moldavia and Wallachia and which had been called for by Count Walewski in 1856 and 1858. From that time on, the Jewish problem was taken up by external forces; punctuated by various interventions, they culminated in 1878 in the Berlin Treaty. In an interval of twenty years, another French diplomat, Waddington, demanded equality in civil and political rights for the Jews. We have seen how Article 44 was applied in Romania. The Western powers, who, one after the other, abandoned the "humanitarian" principles which had guided them in writing the Berlin Treaty, never reached unanimity in opposing the arbitrary Romanian legislation, even in 1902 when the United States urged them to do so in the famous, but timid, Hay Note.

This externalization of the Jewish problem and the role played by Western Jewish organizations exasperated the representatives of Romanian nationalism the most. The internal side of the problem was due to the convergence of several factors which we have analyzed. As in the other countries of Eastern Europe, it seems that the Jews were pursued in Romania "less by religious intolerance than by a kind of national intolerance, a narrow and suspicious patriotism," as Anatole Leroy-Beaulieu expressed it in his book, *Israël chez les nations*, published in Paris in 1823. In fact, this involved a general concept of freedom, described in 1958 by Professor Pierre Guiral as follows: "The deeper one penetrates Eastern Europe, the less freedom is understood and the less it is respected."

The tragic paradox of the Romanian Jews stems from the fact that, while playing a particular economic role, they did not belong to any social class.

Whereas prior to 1878, it was the lack of assimilation which seemed to justify hostility towards the Jews, after that date, it was rather the fear of such assimilation which explains the severe legislative measures taken against them. From a certain point of view, the fate of the Romanian Jews during the last three decades of the nineteenth century confirms one of the laws of Jewish history expressed by Professor J.L. Talmon, namely, that "a new society, regime or economic system allows the Jews to come as pioneers among them, but they dismiss them without ceremony when the natives are ready to replace the Jews in their work."

Considering the actual situation of the Jews in Romania, one must note differences and emphasize that, despite discrimination and ostracism, they formed an important element in the country's economy. Also, in spite of iniquitous laws regarding education, the Jews were not entirely eliminated from the secondary schools and universities. Besides the schools, military service by "foreigners not under foreign protection" was a powerful means of assimilation for the Jewish youth. Aside from explosions of religious fanaticism, good neighborly relations were established between Jews and Christians. However, in spite of certain progress, integration of the Jews was constantly hindered by the attitude of the authorities and the maneuvers of extremist nationalist organizations. It seemed as though the desire of the Jews to blend with the Romanian nation had a boomerang effect: the more they aspired to integration, the less society accepted them.

From the viewpoint of the history of opinions, we must be careful not to draw hasty, subjective and Manichean conclusions, opposing the "good Jew," to the "bad Christian." Undoubtedly that "good Jew," with his meticulous particularism, his desire to remain distinct, while aspiring to participate in the socio-political life of the country, his obstinate refusal to accept either solicitations towards conversion or the temptation of atheism, was at least partly the creator of his own enclave.

Also there is no doubt that the "bad Christians," listening to Sunday sermons, reminded of the "perfidious" Jew, the executioner of Christ, immersed in a climate of medieval myths and a narrow-minded, touchy nationalism, allowed his anti-Jewish growling to roar out.

In Romania, under conditions of non-emancipation in politics and deprivation of many civil rights, anti-Semitism possessed its own remedy, because it only strengthened the feeling of oneness in the Jewish community. Having become "self-conscious pariahs," in the words of Bernard Lazare, the Jewish masses, impoverished by administrative persecution, embraced with enthusiasm the new frondescence of the thousand-year old ideal of the prophets: Messianic Zionism.

BIBLIOGRAPHICAL REFERENCES

This bibliography contains only titles of printed works of a general nature related to the principal topics treated in the present volume. Works specifically related to Romanian history as such and to the Jewish question in Romania in particular, as well as pertinent primary sources, are contained and should be consulted by specialists in the original French edition *Les Juifs en Roumanie (1866-1919): de l'éxclusion à l'émancipation* (Editions de l'Université de Provence, 1978), pp. 331-366.

I. BASIC REFERENCES/WORKS

Dicţionar Enciclopedic Român, vols. I-IV, Bucureşti.

The Jewish Encyclopedia, vols. I-X, New York, 1906.

Encyclopaedia Judaica, vols. I -XVI, Jerusalem, 1972.

II. WORKS ON HISTORICAL METHODOLOGY

Aries, P. *Histoire des populations françaises et de leur attitude devant la vie depuis le XVIIIᵉ siècle*. Paris: Self, 1948.

Bensimon-Donath, D. *Socio-démographie des Juifs de France et d'Algérie*. Paris: P.O.F., 1976.

Burston, W.B. *Principles of History Teaching*. London: Methuen, 1963.

Chaunu, P. *Histoire, science sociale*. Paris: S.E.D.E.S., 1974.

Elton, G.R. *The Practice of History*. Sydney University Press, 1969.

Fohlen, C. "Jean Marczewski, Introduction à l'histoire quantitative," *Revue historique*, avril-juin, 1967.

Furet, F. "Le quantitatif en Histoire," in *Faire de l'Histoire*. Paris: Gallimard, 1974.

Godechot, J. *La grande nation. L'expression révolutionnaire de la France dans le monde de 1789 à 1799*, vols. I-II. Paris: Aubier, 1956.

________. *Les Révolutions*. Paris: PUF, 1963.

Le Roy Ladurie, E. *Le territoire de l'historien*, Paris: Gallimard, 1974.

Marczewski, J. *Introduction à l'histoire quantitative*. Geneva: Librairie Droz, 1965.

Marrou, H.I. "Théorie et pratique de l'Histoire. Troisième chronique de méthodologie historique," *Revue historique*, vol. 89, janvier-mars, 1965, pp. 139-170.

Veyne, P. *Comment on écrit l'Histoire. Essai d'épistémologie*. Paris: Seuil, 1971.

III. Sources on Anti-Semitism

Ackerman, N. and M. Jahoda. "The Dynamic Basis of Anti-Semitic Attitudes," *The Psychoanalytic Quarterly*, XVII, 1948.

________. *Anti-Semitism and Emotional Disorder: A Psychoanalytic Interpretation*. New York, 1950.

Arendt, H. "The Jews as Pariah, a Hidden Tradition," *Jewish Social Studies*, vol. 6, no. 2, 1944.

________. *Sur l'Antisémitisme*. Paris: Calmann-Levy, 1973.

________. *Eichmann in Jerusalem*. London, 1963.

Bettelheim, B. *The Informed Heart*. 1960.

Drumont, E. *La France Juive. Essai d'Histoire contemporaine*, Ed. illustrée. Paris: Librairie Blériot, n.d.

Ettinger, S. *The Conventional and the New in Modern Anti-Semitism.* Jerusalem, 1968.

Grunberger, B. "The Anti-Semitic and the Oedipal Conflict," *The International Journal of Psychoanalysis*, vol. 45, 1965.

Flannery, E. *L'Angoisse des Juifs.* Paris: Mame, 1969. (Original edition: *The Anguish of the Jews.* New York, 1965).

Friedlander, S. *L'Antisémitisme nazi. Histoire d'une psychose collective.* Paris: Seuil, 1971.

Hilberg, R. *The Destruction of the European Jews.* Chicago, 1961.

Isaac, J. *L'antisémitisme a-t-il des racines chrétiennes.* Paris: Fasquelle, 1960.

_____. *L'enseignement du mépris.* Paris: Fasquelle, 1962.

_____. *Genése de l'antisémitisme.* Paris: C. Levy, 1956.

Katz, J. "A State Within a State: A Story of an Anti-Semitic Slogan," *Proceedings*, Israeli Academy of Sciences and Humanities, 1969 and 1970.

Katzburg, N. *Ha-Antišemiut be-Ungaria, 1867-1914.* Tel Aviv, 1969.

Lazare, B. *L'Antisémitisme, son histoire et ses causes.* Paris: Documents et Témiognages, 1969.

Lendvay, P. *L'Antisémitisme sans Juifs.* Paris: Fayard, 1971.

Levaillant, I. "La genése de l'antisémitisme sous la IIIe République," R.E.J., 53, 1907, Actes et Conférences, pp. LXXVI-C.

Leroy-Beaulieu, A. "*L'Antisémitisme.* Paris: Calmann-Levy, 1897.

Lovsky, F. *L'Antisémitisme et mystère d'Israël.* Paris: Albin-Michel, 1955.

Lovsky, F. *L'Antisémitisme chrétien*, Textes choisis et présentés. Paris: Cerf, 1970.

Poliakov, L. *Histoire de l'Antisémitisme*. Vol. I: *Du Christ aux Juifs de Cour*. Vol. II: *De Mahomet aux Marranes*. Vol. III: *De Voltaire à Wagner*. Paris: Calmann-Levy, 1968.

_____. *Le mythe aryen*. Paris: Calmann-Levy, 1971.

_____. *Le Juifs et notre histoire*. Paris: Flammarion, 1973, especially "L'antisémitisme à travers les âges," pp. 11-34.

Simmel, E., editor. *Anti-Semitism: A Social Disease*. New York, 1946.

Sorlin, P. *L'Antisémitisme allemand*. Paris: Flammarion, 1969.

Ullmo, J. "De l'Antisémitisme," *Revue de la pensée juive*, vol. 2, Paris, 1950.

Wawrzinek, K. *Die Entstehung der deutschen Antisemitenpartein, 1875-1890*. Berlin, 1927.

IV. WORKS ON JEWS AND JUDAISM

Dimont, M. "Les mythes de l'histoire juive," *L'information juive*, janvier, 1973.

Dobzynski, Ch. *Le miroir d'un peuple. Anthologie de la poésie yidich (1870-1970)*. Paris: Gallimard, 1971.

Ettinger, S. *Toldot Am Israel me-Mahapekot 1848 ve-ad haqamat medinat Israel*. Jerusalem, 1966.

Gille, B. *Histoire de la maison Rothschild* (2 volumes). Geneva: Librairie Droz, 1965-67.

Guiral, P. *Les Juifs de Marseille en 1808*. Actes du quatre-vingt cinquième Congrès national des Sociétés Savantes, Chambéry-Annecy, 1960.

Katz, J. "A State Within a State: The History of an Anti-Semitic Slogan," *Proceedings*, Israeli Academy of Sciences and Humanities, 1969 and 1970.

_____. "The Jewish National Movement. A Sociological Analysis," *Journal of World History*, UNESCO, vol. XI, 1969.

Laqueur, W. *Histoire du Sionisme*. Paris: Calmann-Levy, 1973.

Leon, A. *La conception matérialiste de la question juive*. Paris: Ed. Pionniers, 1946.

Leroy-Beaulieu, A. *Israël chez les nations*. Paris, 8ᵉ éd., 1893.

Marrus, M.R. *Les Juifs de France à l'époche de l'affaire Dreyfus*. Paris: Calmann-Levy, 1972.

Marx, K. *La question jive*. Paris: Union générale d'éditions, 10/18, 1968.

Rabi, W. *Anatomie du Judaïsme français*. Paris: Ed. de Minuit, 1962.

Scholem, G. *Le messianisme Juif*. Paris: Calmann-Levy, 1971.

V. HISTORICAL STUDIES CONCERNED IN PART WITH ROMANIA

Castellan, G. "Les Etats balkaniques et sud-est européens dans les relations internationales (fin du XVIIIᵉ siècle-XXᵉ siècle)," *Revue historique*, no. 517, janvier-mars, 1976, pp. 43-60.

Guiral, P. *Prévost-Paradol (1829-1870), Pensée et action d'un libéral sous le Second Empire*. Paris: PUF, 1955.

_____. "L'Expansion de l'Europe" in *Histoire Universelle, Encyclopédie de la Pléïade*, Vol. III. Paris, 1958.

Haupt, G. *La Deuxième Internationale*. Paris-La Haye, 1964.

Mantran, R. *Histoire de la Turquie*. Paris: PUF, 1961.

Tibal, A. *Problèmes politiques contemporains de l'Europe Orientale.* Paris: 1930.

Thomson, D. *Europe Since Napoleon.* London: Pellikan, 1960.

VI. HISTORICAL STUDIES CONCERNED IN PART WITH ROMANIAN JEWRY

Bernfeld, M. "Le Sionisme," *Etude de droit international public,* Paris, 1920 (*Roumanie*, pp. 207-225).

Chouraqui, A. *L'Alliance israélite universelle et la renaissance jive contemporaine. Cents ans d'Histoire.* Paris: PUF, 1965 (*La Roumanie*, pp. 87-100).

Dubnov, S. *Histoire moderne du peuple juif.* Paris, 1940. Vol. 1, §20, *La Roumanie et les autres Etats balkaniques*, pp. 201-211; Vol. 2, §40, *La Roumanie anti-juive*, pp. 525-537.

Leven, N. *Cinquante ans d'Histoire, L'Alliance israélite universelle (1860-1910).* Paris: Félix-Alcan, Vol. I (1911); Vol. II (1920). (Vol. I, chpt. II: *Action de l'Alliance israélite en Serbie et en Roumanie*; chpt. IV: *Le Congrès de Berlin*; chpt. VII: *La Roumanie devant le Traité de Berlin*; Vol. II, chpt. XI: *L'Instruction en Roumanie*; chpt. XIII: *L'Emigration des Juifs roumains.*)

Les Juifs en Europe (1939-1945). Paris: Centre de Documentation juive contemporaine, 1949 (*La Roumanie*, pp. 204-207. Rapport de Me. M. Carp).

La persécution des Juifs dans les pays de l'Europe de l'est présentée à Nuremberg. Paris: Centre de Documentation juive contemporaine, 1949 (*La Roumanie*, pp. 258-260).